# CAMBRIDGE

# A Christmas Carol
## GCSE English Literature for AQA
## Student Book

Imelda Pilgrim
*Series editor: Peter Thomas*

# CAMBRIDGE
## UNIVERSITY PRESS

University Printing House, Cambridge CB2 8BS, United Kingdom

Cambridge University Press is part of the University of Cambridge.

It furthers the University's mission by disseminating knowledge in the pursuit of education, learning and research at the highest international levels of excellence.

www.cambridge.org
Information on this title: www.cambridge.org/ukschools/9781316504604 (Paperback)
www.cambridge.org/ukschools/9781316504611 (Cambridge Elevate-enhanced Edition)
www.cambridge.org/ukschools/9781316504666 (Paperback + Cambridge Elevate-enhanced Edition)

First published 2015

Printed in the United Kingdom by Latimer Trend

*A catalogue record for this publication is available from the British Library*

ISBN 978-1-316-50460-4 Paperback
ISBN 978-1-316-50461-1 Cambridge Elevate-enhanced Edition
ISBN 978-1-316-50466-6 Paperback + Cambridge Elevate-enhanced Edition

Additional resources for this publication at www.cambridge.org/ukschools

## Message from AQA

This textbook has been approved by AQA for use with our qualification. This means that we have checked that it broadly covers the specification and we are satisfied with the overall quality. Full details of our approval process can be found on our website.

We approve textbooks because we know how important it is for teachers and students to have the right resources to support their teaching and learning. However, the publisher is ultimately responsible for the editorial control and quality of this book.

Please note that when teaching the GCSE English Literature (8702) course, you must refer to AQA's specification as your definitive source of information. While this book has been written to match the specification, it cannot provide complete coverage of every aspect of the course.

A wide range of other useful resources can be found on the relevant subject pages of our website: www.aqa.org.uk

# Contents

# Introduction

Welcome to your GCSE English Literature for AQA student book on *A Christmas Carol*. This is one of Dickens's best-known stories and we hope you will enjoy it first at GCSE and then later in life. This book will help you get the most out of the novel and do the best you can. It will develop your skills in reading and responding to a 19th-century novel and in writing for GCSE English Literature.

## Part 1: Exploring the novel

Part 1 leads you through *A Christmas Carol*. It ensures you build a thorough understanding of the plot, structure and methods that Dickens used to create a popular and entertaining story for his magazine readers in 1843 – one that has maintained its popularity for 170 years. The units investigate the text, section by section, and provide activities for writing, drama and discussion that will deepen your experience, understanding, interpretations and analysis of the novel. Your work in each unit will provide you with notes and focused responses on aspects of the novel that are important to understand for GCSE.

## Part 2: The novel as a whole

Part 2 provides an overview of key aspects of *A Christmas Carol*, including structure, characterisation and language. It will develop your detailed knowledge and understanding, as well as helping you revise your responses to the novel as a whole.

## Preparing for your exam

The last part of this book gives you practice and guidance in preparing for your exam. It offers examples of answers showing skills at different levels so you can assess your own areas of strength and weakness and focus your efforts to improve accordingly.

We hope that you will enjoy using this resource, not only to support your GCSE English Literature study but also to help you see that 19th-century novels have plenty to say about the life around you – and within you.

*Peter Thomas*
Series Editor

# Introducing
# *A Christmas Carol*

## THE 19TH-CENTURY NOVEL AND *A CHRISTMAS CAROL*

### The 19th-century novel

Dickens wrote in an age long before television and digital media. Cheap printing made books and magazines available to increasing numbers of people. Dickens made a living out of writing novels, but he was not the first to do so. Before him, Jane Austen and Walter Scott had built a loyal readership of their published fiction. William Thackeray – only seven months older than Dickens – was also releasing stories in magazine instalments before publishing them as single-volume novels.

In the 1850s and 1860s, these weekly or monthly magazines were a major source of entertainment. They offered a mixture of news features, articles on crime and accounts of travels. The serial story was a major selling point – readers would queue up to buy the latest instalment, keen to find out how the previous issue's cliff-hanger was resolved.

### Dickens the writer

Charles Dickens was born in 1812 and died in 1870. He is one of the greatest writers of the Victorian period and wrote some of the best-loved novels of all time. Dickens never went to university and even his schooling was interrupted. As a boy he worked in a factory, and he went on to be a journalist before trying his hand at writing stories. For most of his life, Dickens made his living by writing to entertain adults. He wrote for his own magazines, first *Household Words* then *All the Year Round*, both of which offered a mixture of social comment and fiction. As his reputation grew, he built on his success by producing stories designed to appeal to everyone, throwing into the mix elements of romance, humour, mystery, crime and the less glamorous side of life in Britain's great capital, London.

Dickens wrote about 16 novels all together (depending on what you count as a novel), as well as short stories and articles. His books were so successful that he became very wealthy, and he further increased his income by touring the UK and the USA giving readings from his novels. *A Christmas Carol* was written and published in 1843. Dickens wrote his 'little Christmas book', as he called it, in only six weeks – just in time for Christmas.

## Structure and plot

*A Christmas Carol* is divided into five parts:

- Scrooge's miserly existence and the visit of Marley's Ghost
- the visit of the Ghost of Christmas Past
- the visit of the Ghost of Christmas Present
- the visit of the Ghost of Christmas Yet to Come
- Scrooge's new life.

The novel opens and closes with Scrooge talking to his nephew, Fred. At the beginning, Scrooge refuses to keep Christmas and rejects his nephew's invitation to Christmas dinner; at the end of the novel he visits his nephew and asks if he is still welcome. This gives the story a circular structure that reflects one of Dickens's key themes – the development of a man who is taken on a journey of discovery by four ghosts, and who finally understands the things that should be most valued in life.

**Find out more about plot and structure in *A Christmas Carol* in Unit 6.**

## Context and setting

The immediate context of the novel is England in the early to mid-19th century, with scenes set in the city of London. The novel offers a window into Dickens's times, including information about the plight of the poor following the Industrial Revolution. Many people flocked from the countryside to the city in search of work; this work could be hard to find, and even when a job was found it could be extremely badly paid. Scrooge can get away with paying his clerk, Bob Cratchit, a pittance because there are lots of other people who would do that job for the same money.

The wider context is of 19th-century fiction being used not only to entertain the reader, but also to give a realistic insight into the types of people and the institutions that made up society in Dickens's time. This novel is packed with details about the lives of a wide variety of people, and filled with observations of characters in both their private lives and public roles.

**Find out more about context and setting in *A Christmas Carol* in Unit 7.**

## Characterisation

Characters from every walk of life inhabit the novel and Dickens shows great skill in making them all believable. He does this by focusing on details of their appearance, their movements and speech habits, as well as what they actually say and do.

**Find out more about character and characterisation in *A Christmas Carol* in Unit 8.**

## Ideas

Dickens was much concerned with the injustices he saw in the world around him. He shows great sympathy for the poor in 19th-century society, and he empathises with the harshness that many children experienced. He is particularly good when writing about how people manage to keep their optimism in the face of difficulties and drawbacks, and how events often influence the development of someone's personality.

**Find out more about themes and ideas in *A Christmas Carol* in Unit 9.**

## Interpretation

Your own response to the novel matters. What you think of the characters, which parts of the novel make you think or smile, which sections relate to your own experience – all these things will help you write about *A Christmas Carol* in an interesting way. Most important is what the novel means to you when it shows you ways that people behave, and how relationships develop or go wrong.

## Language

Dickens uses narrative text and dialogue with equal skill. His narrative helps to convey realistic impressions of places and people, designed to evoke different emotions in the reader – amusement or sadness, or fear, perhaps. The description of Marley's Ghost, for example, shows how Dickens tries to terrify his readers:

But how much greater was his horror when the phantom, taking off the bandage around his head, as if it were too warm to wear indoors, its lower jaw dropped down onto its breast!

Stave One

Narrative text allows Dickens to involve his reader; he uses a conversational style to address his reader directly so that they feel involved in the story:

You will, therefore, permit me to repeat, emphatically, that Marley was as dead as a doornail. Scrooge knew he was dead? Of course he did. How could it be otherwise?

Stave One

⟷ **Find out more about language in *A Christmas Carol* in Unit 10.**

# Marley was as dead as a doornail.

*Stave One*

## THE 19TH-CENTURY NOVEL AND GCSE ENGLISH LITERATURE

Your GCSE English Literature course has been designed to include a range of drama, prose and poetry. *A Christmas Carol* is a great story, thought-provoking and political, as the reader sees a cruel man transformed.

At the end of your GCSE course in English Literature you will sit an exam. This is made up of two papers:

- **Paper 1: Shakespeare and the 19th-century novel**. This is worth 40% of your GCSE English Literature.
- **Paper 2: Modern texts and poetry**. This is worth 60% of your GCSE English Literature.

In Paper 1, there are two sections:

- **Section A: Shakespeare**. You will answer one question on the play you have studied. You will be required to write in detail about an extract from the play and then to write about the play as a whole.
- **Section B: The 19th-century novel**. You will answer one question on the novel you have studied – *A Christmas Carol*. You will be required to write in detail about an extract from the novel and then to write about the novel as a whole.

## GCSE ENGLISH LITERATURE ASSESSMENT OBJECTIVES

The assessment objectives form the basis for the GCSE English Literature mark scheme. Your answer in Paper 1, Section B (the 19th-century novel) will be read by an examiner who will be guided by these assessment objectives, as follows:

**AO1:** Read, understand and respond to texts. Students should be able to:

- maintain a critical style and develop an informed personal response
- use textual references, including quotations, to support and illustrate interpretations.

**AO2:** Analyse the language, form and structure used by a writer to create meanings and effects, using relevant subject terminology where appropriate.

**AO3:** Show understanding of the relationships between texts and the contexts in which they were written.

### Learning checkpoint

The assessment objectives mean that in your GCSE English Literature exams you need to show that you:

✔ understand what has been written
✔ have formed opinions about the book and are able to express them
✔ understand how the language makes things seem real, interesting or frightening
✔ have something to say about the form the writing takes and how it is structured
✔ have some sense of context for the events in the book, the time it was written and how it may be relevant today
✔ can support your arguments and opinions by quoting the novel itself.

## LITERATURE SKILLS AND STUDY FOCUS AREAS

During your course of study you will develop the core skills to show understanding, interpretation and analysis. These, along with the following study areas, give a focus for your work in this book.

### Ideas, attitudes and feelings

You will be expected to understand and respond to the feelings, ideas or attitudes expressed in the novel. These three things all relate to **content**:

- **Ideas** are the thoughts that explain or result from an experience.
- **Attitudes** are the positions or postures adopted when facing experiences.
- **Feelings** are the emotions people experience, which are often quite different from their attitudes and ideas.

For example you could say that:

- an **idea** expressed in A Christmas Carol is that there is a huge gap between the lives of the rich and the poor
- an **attitude** we see in A Christmas Carol is that those who have more than others are duty bound to help those less well-off, especially at Christmas, and that Scrooge's attitude is wrong
- we **feel** sad at the thought of the Cratchits suffering at Christmas; we **feel** anger at Scrooge's selfishness.

### The writer's methods

You will also be expected to understand and respond to the way in which the novel is written – the writer's methods. The writer uses language, form and structure to enable him to convey his message more effectively to the reader. Again, these are three distinct things. In the case of A Christmas Carol, for example, you could say that:

- **language** can be used to set the scene – for example in the quotation '**Foggier yet, and colder! Piercing, searching, biting cold**', adjectives are used to create a sense of bitter cold
- the **form** is a novella – a short novel
- the **structure** is the way in which the ideas are organised – in A Christmas Carol, the main character is with his nephew at the beginning and the end, to show how he has changed throughout the story; the story is also structured in three main sections, showing Scrooge's past, present and future life, and this shift in time allows him to see the error of his ways, and lets the reader chart Scrooge's development as a character.

## Written response skills

Skill levels at GCSE English Literature can be simplified into three broad categories: understanding, explaining and conceptualising. This book will help you identify your current skill level and show you how to improve.

Throughout this book, you will find examples to help you develop your responses to the novel. They show how you can develop from basic comments (those that are relevant and include a supporting quotation) to using your skills in understanding and interpretation to explain feelings, motives or reasons, and to include ideas that develop and extend meaning. The following are examples of each type of response.

### Understanding

'A Christmas Carol' is a story about a miserly nasty man who changes into a kind and generous man because four ghosts come to visit him. They show him what his life has been like, what it is like now and what it will be like if he doesn't change his ways. He is horrified by what the ghosts show him and decides to be kinder to his fellow man in future.

### Explaining

'A Christmas Carol' is a story about a man who changes his ways because of four visits from four ghosts. If it were not for the visits from the ghosts he would have continued as he was before: being nasty and cruel to his staff; being rude to his family, and refusing to contribute to charities. The novel shows the development of the character of Scrooge.

### Conceptualising

'A Christmas Carol' is a political novel. Dickens uses the story of a miserly old man who has to be frightened out of his old ways by four ghosts to show the corruption at the heart of man and the effects of the Industrial Revolution. Scrooge is reaping the benefits of social and political change by keeping his clerk on low wages and refusing to contribute to charities; Dickens shows us that it takes a visit from the forces of the supernatural to make Scrooge accept his responsibilities both as an employer and as a human being.

## Writing with focus

Each unit helps you develop focused writing skills, so you can be confident about writing in timed conditions in your exam. Be prepared to show how Dickens builds Scrooge's character and uses other characters to provide humour and insight into work, dreams and life – all of which are part of the novel's rich depiction of life in England in the mid-19th century. Your responses should make your points quickly, link to specific details from the text and show a clear purpose.

## DICKENS AND YOU

We hope your reading of this novel sheds more light onto a very famous story – a story you probably already know. It is one of the most famous tales in English literature and has been adapted into many productions. Your reading will help you to understand what a political novel it is, and that far from being a simple Christmas story, it is a comment on what life was like in 19th-century England.

# 1

## Stave One: Marley's Ghost

### How does Dickens set up the story?

Your progress in this unit:

Your progress in this unit:
- discuss what you already know of the story
- understand the role of the narrator
- examine how Scrooge and Marley's Ghost are presented
- consider ideas about poverty.

### GETTING STARTED – THE STORY AND YOU

#### What's it all about?

Even if you have never read *A Christmas Carol*, you are probably familiar with the story, which has been produced many times on film and television.

**1** Work in small groups. Talk about:

   **a**  any productions of *A Christmas Carol* you have seen
   **b**  what you know about the story.

**2** In your groups, decide which of the following statements about *A Christmas Carol* are true:

   **a**  It is set in New York.
   **b**  Scrooge is visited by four ghosts.
   **c**  The ghosts appear on New Year's Eve.
   **d**  The story was written by Walt Disney.
   **e**  It is set in London.
   **f**  Scrooge always carries a pocket watch.
   **g**  Three ghosts appear before Scrooge.
   **h**  It was written in the 19th century.
   **i**  Scrooge falls into his own grave.
   **j**  It ends with the words 'God bless us, every one!'

The story is divided into five 'staves', or chapters. A stave is a musical symbol made up of five horizontal lines and four spaces, which each represent a different musical pitch. Dickens may have chosen to call his chapters 'staves' to reflect the title *A Christmas Carol*, with its **connotations** of songs and music. The story was first published in 1843. It is set in Victorian England, at Christmas time.

Read the summary, then read Stave One.

> **Watch a dramatic reading of the beginning of Stave One on Cambridge Elevate.**

### GETTING CLOSER – FOCUS ON DETAILS

#### The meaning of Christmas

**1** Work in small groups. Talk about:

   **a**  what Christmas means to you
   **b**  whether you celebrate Christmas or not
   **c**  the traditions you associate with Christmas.

> **Key terms**
>
> **connotations:** things or ideas suggested by a word.

## STAVE ONE: MARLEY'S GHOST

It is Christmas Eve. Scrooge is busy in his counting-house, keeping a careful eye on his clerk, Bob Cratchit. Scrooge's nephew arrives to wish him a Merry Christmas and invite him to dinner the next day. Scrooge rudely refuses the invitation.

As the nephew leaves, two portly gentlemen arrive and ask Scrooge to donate to a fund to help the poor. Scrooge refuses and turns the gentlemen away. The next visitor is a young carol singer who is quickly frightened away by Scrooge's actions.

As the day moves on, the fog and darkness thicken and it becomes colder. When it is time to close the counting-house, Scrooge scolds his clerk for wanting Christmas Day off work.

Scrooge eats in a tavern and makes his solitary way home. When he arrives, he notes with some alarm that his door knocker appears to have changed into the face of his former business partner, Jacob Marley, who has been dead for seven years.

Scrooge enters his house cautiously, checking that all is as it should be before double locking his door, putting on his nightgown and sitting down by a small fire to eat his gruel. Suddenly, every bell in the house begins to ring and he hears the clanking of chains. Marley's Ghost appears.

At first, Scrooge claims not to believe in this ghostly figure, but its fearful cry soon changes his mind. Marley's Ghost explains that the heavy chain it carries was formed throughout Marley's lifetime when he failed to help others. The ghost tells Scrooge that his own chain is growing even longer and heavier.

Marley's Ghost explains that Scrooge will be visited by three spirits. These spirits will give him a chance to avoid Marley's fate. After showing Scrooge many other ghosts as a warning, Marley's Ghost leaves and Scrooge goes to bed.

**2** The following quotations are taken from Stave One. How far do they reflect your own experiences of Christmas?

a **Greetings:** 'A Merry Christmas, uncle! God save you!'

b **Cost:** 'What's Christmastime to you but a time for paying bills without money?'

c **Charity:** 'I have always thought of Christmastime […] as a good time; a kind, forgiving, charitable, pleasant time.'

d **Food:** 'Come! Dine with us tomorrow.'

e **Shopping:** The brightness of the shops, where holly sprigs and berries crackled in the lamp heat of the windows …

f **Carols:** 'God bless you, merry gentleman, / May nothing you dismay!'

## Ideas about charity

The idea of charity is important in *A Christmas Carol*. Look at this dictionary definition of 'charity':

---

**charity** *noun* (giving)

1 a system of giving money, food, or help free to those who are in need because they are ill, poor or have no home, or any organisation that has the purpose of providing money or helping in this way.

2 the quality of being kind to people and not judging them in a severe way.

---

**1** Talk about:

a your views on helping the poor

b the importance of charity at Christmas

c the importance of showing kindness to others.

**2** The chain that Marley's Ghost carries was not created by the bad things he did in life, but by his failure to do good. In Stave One, what opportunities has Scrooge had – and failed to use – to do good?

**3** Scrooge's famous expression is '**Humbug!**' Use a dictionary to find out what this word means. What does Scrooge's frequent use of this word suggest about his attitude to the world?

## Dickens's purpose

'Who **tells** this story?' is not the same question as 'Who **wrote** this story?' We know that Charles Dickens wrote *A Christmas Carol*. In a short **preface**, he reveals the effect he hoped it would have on his readers:

I have endeavoured in this Ghostly little book to raise the Ghost of an Idea, which shall not put my readers out of humour with themselves, with each other, with the season, or with me. May it haunt their houses pleasantly and no one wish to lay it.

*Preface*

**1** What effects does he hope the story will and will not have on his readers?

**2** Choose words from the word bank to describe the **tone** of this preface. Explain your choices.

| | | |
|---|---|---|
| sinister | mysterious | playful |
| light-hearted | frightening | serious |

## The narrator

The **narrator** is the person who tells the story. There are different types of narrative, including **first-person narrative** and **third-person narrative**. In *A Christmas Carol*, Dickens combines these two.

The narrator uses the first-person narrative:

Mind! I don't mean to say that I know, of my own knowledge, what there is particularly dead about a doornail.

*Stave One*

He makes judgements about the **characters**:

External heat and cold had little influence on Scrooge. No warmth could warm, no wintry weather chill him. No wind that blew was bitterer than he.

*Stave One*

He addresses the reader directly:

You will, therefore, permit me to repeat, emphatically, that Marley was dead as a doornail.

*Stave One*

However, large parts of *A Christmas Carol* are written in the third person:

The Lord Mayor, in the stronghold of the mighty Mansion House, gave orders to his fifty cooks and butlers to keep Christmas as a Lord Mayor's household should.

*Stave One*

**1** Copy the following table. Find further examples in Stave One to support the statements made in the first column.

| The narrator … | Evidence |
|---|---|
| uses the first-person narrative | |
| makes judgements about the characters | |
| addresses the reader directly | |
| sees and knows everything | |
| uses the third-person narrative | |

### 🔑 Key terms

**preface:** an introduction or explanation written by the author at the start of a book.

**tone:** the mood or attitude that a writer conveys in a story.

**narrator:** the character in a novel who tells the story.

**first-person narrative:** an account of events using the pronouns 'I', 'me' and 'we'.

**third-person narrative:** an account of events using 'he', 'she' or 'they', rather than 'I' or 'we'.

**characters:** the people in a story; even when based on real people, characters in a novel are invented or fictionalised.

## The listener

In Victorian times, people often listened to stories being read to them. This may explain why the narrator in *A Christmas Carol* sometimes sounds as though he is speaking aloud, and why Dickens sometimes uses punctuation in an unusual and non-standard way.

**1** Work in small groups. Focus on the first nine paragraphs of Stave One, where the narrator reveals Scrooge's history with Marley – up to the words '**Once upon a time**'. Take it in turn to read a paragraph aloud. Aim to:

  **a** capture the 'voice' of the narrator
  **b** engage your listeners through your tone and expression.

**2** Talk about the ways in which this narrator seems to see and know everything. Focus on:

  **a** what he knows about past events
  **b** what he reveals about Scrooge
  **c** what he reveals about how others respond to Scrooge.

## PUTTING DETAILS TO USE

### Describing Scrooge

Dickens created many well-known characters, but Ebenezer Scrooge is one of his most famous. The word 'Scrooge' even appears in dictionaries and is associated with being mean or miserly.

We learn about Scrooge's life, his actions, his thoughts and words through the story's narrator. At times, the narrator makes judgements on Scrooge, but sometimes he leaves readers to judge for themselves. Right from the start, we get a clear idea of the narrator's view of Scrooge: '**Oh! but he was a tight-fisted hand at the grindstone, Scrooge!**' Read the full paragraph. You may find the following explanations of some of the words useful:

- **grindstone:** a round solid stone used for sharpening knives and tools
- **covetous:** eagerly or enviously wanting things
- **flint:** a very hard mineral that produces a spark when struck
- **oyster:** a mollusc that lives in a hard shell
- **gait:** way of walking
- **rime:** ice formed by droplets of fog
- **dog days:** the hottest days of the year.

**Find out more about plot and structure in *A Christmas Carol* in Unit 6.**

### Contexts

School attendance was not made compulsory until 1870 – 27 years after *A Christmas Carol* was published. Many people in Victorian England could not read and there was no radio or television. Instead, adults and children alike would listen to stories being read aloud to them. Dickens was well aware of this, of course, so he wrote his stories with the listener in mind, as well as the reader.

**1** Look at the following table, which identifies some of the language features in this paragraph. Copy the table and complete it by explaining the effect of each language feature.

| Quotation | Language feature | Effect |
|---|---|---|
| 'a squeezing, wrenching, grasping, scraping, clutching, covetous, old sinner' | a list of seven **adjectives** used to describe Scrooge the 'sinner' | |
| 'Hard and sharp as flint from which no steel had ever struck out generous fire' | extended **simile** | |
| 'solitary as an oyster' | simile | |

**2** List all the words and phrases in this paragraph that link to coldness. What do these add to your impression of Scrooge?

**3** Now read the next paragraph. How does Dickens use aspects of the weather to continue the description of Scrooge?

**4** What do you think the final sentence of this paragraph means?

⇄ **Find out more about language in *A Christmas Carol* in Unit 10.**

🔑 **Key terms**

**adjective:** a word that describes a person, place or thing.
**simile:** a comparison between two things that uses the words 'as' or 'like'.

Oh! but he was a tight-fisted hand at the grindstone, Scrooge!

*Stave One*

### How Scrooge interacts with others

The narrator describes how Scrooge liked '**to edge his way along the crowded paths of life, warning all human sympathy to keep its distance**'.

**1** What does this suggest about how Scrooge interacts with other people?

In Stave One, there are several examples of how Scrooge relates to other people. While working in his counting-house, he is visited by his nephew, two portly gentlemen and a carol singer. The narrator allows readers to judge Scrooge for themselves.

**2** Create three spider diagrams to show the details of each visit. Use this sample as a template:

what you learn about the visitor(s)

The visitor(s)

what the visitor(s) wants

how Scrooge responds

**Find out more about character and characterisation in A Christmas Carol in Unit 8.**

**3** Scrooge also interacts with his clerk. Think about how Scrooge treats him and make notes on:

a    the fire he is allowed
b    how much he is paid
c    Scrooge's attitude to his clerk having Christmas Day off work.

**4** Write a paragraph in which you explain what kind of man Scrooge is to someone who has not read the book. Use evidence from the text to support the points you make.

### Building tension

The first words Scrooge speaks in Stave One are '**Bah! Humbug!**' When he sees Marley's face on his fireplace tiles, he says '**Humbug!**' and when he hears the clanking of Marley's chain, he says '**It's humbug still!**' At the end of Stave One, however, '**he tried to say "Humbug!" but stopped at the first syllable**'.

**1** Write a few sentences explaining why you think Scrooge is unable to say 'Humbug'.

**2** Focus on the part of the text after Marley's Ghost appears. Place the following events in the correct order:

a   The ghost removes its bandage.
b   The ghost regrets the life it lived.
c   Scrooge invites Marley's Ghost to sit down.
d   Scrooge sees other chain-bound phantoms.
e   Scrooge tries to crack a joke.
f   The ghost explains why it wears a chain.
g   Scrooge goes straight to bed.
h   The ghost tells Scrooge it has come to save him.
i   Marley's Ghost appears.
j   The ghost tells Scrooge he will be haunted by three spirits.

## The importance of Marley's Ghost

Dickens opens his story with the statement: **'Marley was dead, to begin with'**. Even so, the title of Stave One – 'Marley's Ghost' – suggests that we are going to find out a lot more about him. As the stave unfolds, this proves to be the case. He is the first ghost we see and he sows the seeds of doubt in Scrooge's mind about the kind of person he is.

**1** How many references are there to the death of Marley in the first four paragraphs? List as many as you can find.

**2** **'Scrooge was his sole executor, his sole administrator, his sole assign, his sole residuary legatee, his sole friend, and sole mourner, And even Scrooge was not so dreadfully cut up by the sad event.'** What does this tell you about Marley?

After describing the history of Scrooge and Marley, Dickens brings the narrative forward to relate the events that take place on this particular Christmas Eve. It is only when Scrooge returns home that Marley reappears in the tale.

**3** Answer the following questions to explore how Dickens builds the tension in this part of the story.

a   When Scrooge puts the key in his door he sees Marley's face in the knocker. Note down five features of this face.
b   What does Scrooge think he sees on the staircase?
c   What precautions does Scrooge take before he shuts his door?
d   List three other strange things that happen before the cellar door flies open.

**4** What effect does the description of the cellar door flying open have on the reader?

## Picturing Marley's Ghost

Dickens creates a clear picture of Marley's Ghost in the reader's mind.

**1** In some ways, the ghost resembles the man Marley was when he was alive. In other ways, it is very different.

a   What is the ghost wearing?
b   What binds its head and chin?
c   Can Scrooge see through it?
d   What adjectives does Dickens use to describe its eyes?
e   Why are its hair and clothes **'bristling'**?

**2** What items form the ghost's chain? Why do you think the chain is made of these items?

**3** What is the effect of the following descriptions in the text?

a   the ghost's reaction to Scrooge's **'Humbug'**
b   what happens when the ghost removes its bandage.

## The ghost's message

Marley's Ghost has a message for Scrooge. Once Scrooge says that he believes in what he sees, Marley explains that the spirit within every man has a duty to 'travel far and wide'. By this he means that people should involve themselves with others and – where possible – bring them happiness. If people do not do this, they are doomed to wander helplessly in death.

**1** Find evidence to support the following statements about the purpose and message of Marley's Ghost.

    **a** When Scrooge dies, he will carry a heavier chain than Marley.

    **b** Business and trade should not distract a man from good works.

    **c** Scrooge will be visited at different times by three spirits.

    **d** Chain-carrying phantoms want to help those who are alive.

## The theme of poverty

When Scrooge's nephew wishes him Merry Christmas, Scrooge says: '**What reason have you to be merry? You're poor enough.**' Scrooge regards his nephew as poor, but it is clear that there are different levels of poverty. Scrooge's nephew has enough money to invite his uncle to dine on Christmas Day. Bob Cratchit is poor, but he has a job and is paid 15 shillings a week. Others are very poor and could end up in the workhouse or prison.

**1** Poverty is an important **theme** in *A Christmas Carol*. Read the discussion between the two portly gentlemen and Scrooge. What does it reveal about:

    **a** the number of poor people there were at the time

    **b** the attitude of the two portly gentlemen towards them?

**2** What do we learn about Scrooge's attitude to the poor from:

    **a** what he says about the prisons, workhouses, the treadmill and the Poor Law

    **b** his reference to making '**idle people merry**' and already helping to '**support the establishments**'

    **c** his view that if the poor would rather die '**they had better do it, and decrease the surplus population**'?

**3** Scrooge and the two gentlemen have different perspectives on poverty and charity. Which viewpoint do you think is closest to Dickens's own? Explain why you think this.

### ✔ Learning checkpoint

Imagine that Scrooge is on trial. The prosecution lawyer begins: 'Ebenezer Scrooge, you stand accused of failing to make the common welfare your business.' Find evidence in Stave One to support this accusation. Your evidence should be based on:

✔ things that Scrooge does

✔ things that he says

✔ things that others reveal about him.

Compare your evidence with that of another student and add any points you have missed.

Discuss and make a note of any evidence that could be used to defend Scrooge. Basing your answer on your evidence, would you find Scrooge innocent or guilty?

### Find out more about attitudes to poverty on Cambridge Elevate.

### Key terms

**theme:** an idea that a writer keeps returning to, exploring it from different perspectives.

## Contexts

In 1834, nine years before *A Christmas Carol* was first published, the Poor Law Amendment Act was passed by parliament. Before the act, each parish had to look after its own poor and if someone was unable to work, they were given some money to help them survive. After the act was passed, however, parishes were grouped into 'unions' and each union had to build a workhouse to house the very poor. These workhouses were governed by strict rules and regulations. Families were split up and men and women kept separate. They were dressed poorly and given very little food in exchange for several hours of manual labour each day. Only the most desperate people would go to the workhouse.

Many new prisons were built in the early 19th century and children as well as adults ended up in prison for quite minor offences. Prison life was very difficult and treadmills, or treadwheels, were used for punishment. Prisoners did ten minutes on and five off for eight hours; they climbed the equivalent of around 2,500 metres in the process.

## Further references to poverty

As the stave continues, Dickens makes it clear to the reader that Scrooge's viewpoint is one he will come to regret.

1. The carol singer is described as being '**gnawed and mumbled by the hungry cold as bones are gnawed by dogs**'. What effect does Dickens's use of adjectives and a simile have here?

2. Towards the end of Stave One, one of the phantom figures cries '**piteously**' because he could not help a poor woman and her child. What point do you think Dickens is emphasising here?

3. Marley explains that during his life he should have given more attention to '**charity, mercy, forbearance, and benevolence**'. Look up these words in a dictionary and write a definition of each one.

**Find out more about themes and ideas in *A Christmas Carol* in Unit 9.**

## GETTING IT INTO WRITING

### Writing about Stave One

**1** Look at the two questions in the following table. List the details you would include in an answer to each question. Give examples from the text where possible.

| Question A | Question B |
|---|---|
| What have you learnt about how Scrooge treats other people from reading Stave One? | What have you learnt about Scrooge's attitude to the poor from reading Stave One? |
|  |  |
|  |  |

**2** Look at the following question. Write down any additional details and examples you would use to give a full answer.

**Question C: What have you learnt about Scrooge from reading Stave One?**

**3** Compare your answers to Questions 1 and 2 with those of other students. Add or delete details if you need to.

**4** Copy and complete the following table to plan a response to the two questions.

| Question D | Question E |
|---|---|
| What does Marley's Ghost look like? | Why does Marley's Ghost visit Scrooge? |
|  |  |
|  |  |

**5** Now think about Question F, which requires a more wide-ranging answer.

**Question F: What is the significance of Marley's Ghost in Stave One?**

**a** What details from your table would you include in an answer?

**b** What additional details would you include to answer the question fully?

✓ **Complete this assignment on Cambridge Elevate.**

## GETTING FURTHER

### References to Shakespeare

In Stave One, Dickens refers to Shakespeare's play *Hamlet*. The story would have been familiar to Victorian readers.

- Hamlet's father, the king of Denmark, dies before the play begins, but he appears to Hamlet as a ghost in Act 1 of the play.
- The ghost reveals that he was killed by his brother, Hamlet's uncle.
- Hamlet's uncle now rules Denmark and is married to Hamlet's mother.
- The ghost of Hamlet's father is often shown appearing on the ramparts of his castle.
- This dramatic revelation affects everything that follows in the play.

**1** Why do you think the narrator makes such a detailed reference to *Hamlet* at the start of *A Christmas Carol*?

The air was filled with phantoms, wandering hither and thither in restless haste.

*Stave One*

# 2

## Stave Two: The First of the Three Spirits

### How does the story develop?

Your progress in this unit:
- discuss the significance of Scrooge's memories
- examine the characteristics of the Ghost of Christmas Past
- examine and analyse Dickens's style of writing
- explore the impact the visions of the past have on Scrooge.

## GETTING STARTED – THE STORY AND YOU

### Memories of past times

Marley's Ghost tells Scrooge that he will be visited by three spirits. The first of these is the Ghost of Christmas Past. Memories of people, places and events long forgotten are reawakened in Scrooge as the spirit transports him back to his childhood and youth.

**1** Work in small groups. Take it in turns to describe your earliest memory. Give as much detail as you can remember.

**2** Discuss each of the following quotations relating to memory. Which quotations most closely reflect your own ideas about the importance of memories?

   **a** 'Nothing is ever really lost to us as long as we remember it.' (L.M. Montgomery)

   **b** 'Memory is the diary we all carry about with us.' (Oscar Wilde)

   **c** 'There is no greater sorrow than to recall in misery the time when we were happy.' (Dante Alighieri)

**3** As the Ghost of Christmas Past shows Scrooge, memories of childhood can be happy or sad. Choose another memory from your own childhood. Make notes on what happened and its importance to you.

Read the summary, then read Stave Two.

## GETTING CLOSER – FOCUS ON DETAILS

### Understanding Scrooge

In Stave One, Scrooge is shown as a bitter and mean old man. In Stave Two, however, we realise that there is more to this **character** than first appears.

**1** Find two or three pieces of evidence in Stave Two which suggest that Scrooge once had the capacity to love others and to enjoy life.

**2** Why do you think Scrooge '**seemed uneasy in his mind**' when the Ghost of Christmas Past reminds him that his sister Fan had a child – his nephew?

**3** As Scrooge observes Belle's daughter, his '**sight grew very dim**'. What does this suggest to you?

Scrooge wakes up. He hears the clock chime 12 times and is confused, because he went to bed after 2 a.m. He wonders if he has slept through a whole day and whether Marley's Ghost was just a dream. He lies awake until the clock strikes one, whereupon '**lights flashed**' and the '**curtains of his bed were drawn**' to reveal a '**strange figure**'. A jet of light streams from its head and, under its arm, it carries a cap that could put out the light. This is the Ghost of Christmas Past.

The ghost tells Scrooge that its business is Scrooge's '**welfare**' and '**reclamation**'. It takes Scrooge back in time to the countryside where he grew up and then to the school he attended. The other boys had gone home for '**jolly holidays**', but Scrooge spent Christmases alone, with only his books for company. The scenes reawaken long-forgotten feelings of joy and sadness in Scrooge, and he is delighted when his sister, Fan, comes to take him '**home for good**'.

Scrooge is next taken to the warehouse where he was apprenticed as a young man to old Fezziwig, who held a ball for his employees on Christmas Eve. Scrooge is delighted by what the ghost shows him, and he starts to express some regret at how he treated the carol singer, his nephew and Bob Cratchit earlier in the day.

The next scene is not a happy one. Scrooge is older and '**begins to wear the signs of care**'. His fiancée, Belle, is freeing him from their contract because '**another idol has displaced**' her (Scrooge's passion for making money). Scrooge begs to be shown '**no more**', but one final scene awaits him. The ghost shows him the loving family home in which Belle now lives with her husband and children.

Scrooge can bear no more. Seizing the cap, he places it over the spirit's head to put out the light. However, even though the ghost drops beneath it, Scrooge cannot '**hide the light**'. Now back in his own bedroom, Scrooge sinks into a heavy sleep.

### Describing the Ghost of Christmas Past

The Ghost of Christmas Past is the first of the three spirits Scrooge was told about by Marley's Ghost. Dickens describes this spirit in some detail.

**1** Create a 'brief' for an artist working on an illustrated edition of *A Christmas Carol* to help them draw a picture of the Ghost of Christmas Past.

    **a** List all the details about the ghost's appearance that are mentioned in the text.

    **b** Decide which features would be essential to show in a drawing, and which features might be difficult to show.

    **c** Share your decisions with a partner and discuss any differences of opinion.

    **d** Change your brief if necessary to make it as clear and helpful as possible.

**2** Look at the description of the ghost's body:

… of which dissolving parts, no outline would be visible in the dense gloom wherein they melted away. And, in the very wonder of this, it would be itself again; distinct and clear as ever.

Stave Two

To what extent could this description also be applied to memories of the past?

### Characteristics of the ghost

Marley's Ghost is quite noisy: it has clanking chains and can raise '**a fearful cry**'. The Ghost of Christmas Past is a different sort of spirit.

**1** How does the Ghost of Christmas Past treat Scrooge? Is it harsh or gentle? Find five short quotations from the text to back up your ideas.

**2** Explain, using examples from the text, how this spirit seems to be:

    **a** prepared to challenge Scrooge

    **b** determined to show him all he needs to see.

### The ghost's light and cap

Two of the ghost's most notable features are the light that springs from the top of its head and the cap it holds under its arm, which could put out that '**bright clear jet of light**'. After Fezziwig's ball, '**the light upon its head burnt very clear**'. Near the end of Stave Two '**its light was burning high and bright**'. Dickens may be using the light and the cap as **symbols** to visually represent something.

**1** Do you agree with this interpretation? Why, or why not?

**2** Look at the following suggestions for what the light might represent. Find evidence from the text to support each one.

    **a**   The light represents memory.

    **b**   The light represents the need for people to remember their past.

    **c**   The light represents the need for people to learn from their past.

**3** At the end of Stave Two, Scrooge '**could not hide the light**'. What does this suggest to you?

> Watch Scrooge being interviewed about the ghost on Cambridge Elevate.

> Find out more about character and characterisation in *A Christmas Carol* in Unit 8.

## PUTTING DETAILS TO USE

### Creating a sense of excitement

Scrooge is delighted to revisit the warehouse where he was apprenticed and even more so to see the re-enactment of old Fezziwig's ball on Christmas Eve. Dickens uses a range of different techniques to create this joyful scene, filled with lively activity.

Dickens often uses lists to create a sense of excitement and fun:

---

He rubbed his hands; adjusted his capacious waistcoat; laughed all over himself, from his shoes to his organ of benevolence; and called out, in a comfortable, oily, rich, fat, jovial voice.

---

Stave Two

verbs used to describe Fezziwig's actions
adjectives used to describe Fezziwig's voice
semi-colons used to separate details in the list

Here, the verbs indicate old Fezziwig's actions. The unusual phrase '**laughed all over himself**' suggests that every part of his body reflects good humour. The list of **adjectives** used to describe his voice suggests a contented, wealthy and happy man.

**1** Read the following quotation. Copy it out, then annotate it to show:

    **a**   the verbs used to describe actions

    **b**   how Dickens creates a sense of speed

    **c**   the effect of the **simile** at the end.

---

They charged into the street with the shutters – one, two, three – had 'em up in their places – four, five, six – barred 'em and pinned 'em – seven, eight, nine – and came back before you could have got to twelve, panting like race-horses.

---

Stave Two

**2** Look at the long sentence that describes how the apprentices packed things away to make room for the guests at the ball. What actions are listed at the start of the sentence? What is the effect of this list?

**3** Dickens completes the sentence with another list.

    **a**   What adjectives are listed to describe the warehouse?

    **b**   Why do you think Dickens chose these adjectives?

> **Key terms**
>
> **symbol:** an object used to represent something else.

## Analyse a paragraph

Dickens sometimes uses long paragraphs to build up detail. These paragraphs are carefully structured to help the reader picture a scene.

**1** Find an example of a long paragraph in Stave Two. Identify the following features in the paragraph you have chosen:

    **a** what Dickens starts with
    **b** what he moves on to
    **c** any shift in focus
    **d** how the paragraph ends.

**2** Read the following quotation:

> In they all came, one after another; some shyly, some boldly, some gracefully, some awkwardly, some pushing, some pulling; in they all came, anyhow and everyhow.

Stave Two

Explain the effect of the list in this sentence.

**3** In pairs, talk about what the following simile and **metaphor** suggest to you:

    **a** The fiddler tuned his fiddle '**like fifty long stomach aches**'.
    **b** '**In came Mrs Fezziwig, one vast substantial smile.**'

### ✔ Learning checkpoint

In pairs, discuss and make notes on the techniques Dickens uses to describe the ball scene in Stave Two. Focus on:

✔ the use of lists
✔ the use of punctuation
✔ any other techniques you have noticed.

Share your ideas with a partner. Add to your notes if you need to.

## Shadows of the things that have been

The Ghost of Christmas Past guides Scrooge through his childhood memories, on to when he was a young apprentice and later when he was '**a man in the prime of his life**'. It shows him six distinct scenes from the past. Each of these visions of the past has an effect on Scrooge.

In the first scene from the past, the ghost shows Scrooge the place where he grew up, where he sees boys he knew on their way home for Christmas. The Ghost then shows him a second, more painful scene from this period of his life: he sees himself left alone at school at Christmas.

**1** Copy and complete the following table to show what you think Scrooge's responses to these memories means.

| Memory | Scrooge's response | What might Scrooge's response mean? |
| --- | --- | --- |
| 'a thousand odours floating in the air' | His lip trembles and he seems to have a tear on his cheek. | |
| the route | He recognises every gate, and post and tree. | |
| the boys travelling home | He rejoiced and his heart 'leapt up' as they passed. | |
| the boys wishing each other Merry Christmas | He was filled with gladness. | |

**2** Find evidence to suggest that:

**a** Scrooge was saddened by the second scene the ghost showed him

**b** as a boy, reading was a joyful escape from loneliness for Scrooge.

**3** What does Scrooge wish at the end of this vision?

**Key terms**

**metaphor:** a type of comparison that describes one thing as if it was another.

In came Mrs Fezziwig, one vast substantial smile.

*Stave Two*

## Scrooge's sister

In the third scene from his past, time moves on to a later Christmas. Once again, Scrooge is alone at school. The door opens and a little girl enters. This is his sister, Fan, who has come to take him home. We already know that Scrooge has a nephew. Here, more is revealed about his family.

**1** Create a spider diagram to show the different things that are revealed about Fan in Stave Two. Include details relating to:

   **a**  her appearance
   **b**  her relationships with her brother and her father
   **c**  the kind of person she is
   **d**  her adult life
   **e**  how Scrooge responds to this memory of his sister.

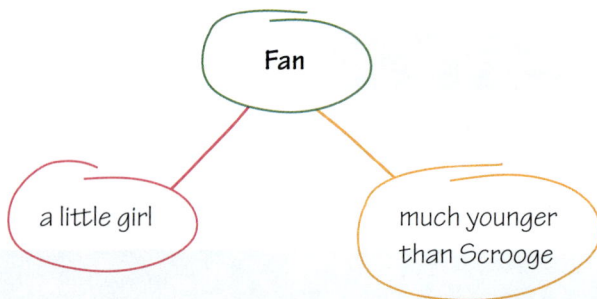

Fan — a little girl — much younger than Scrooge

## Memories of youth

For the fourth visit to the past, the ghost transports Scrooge to the place of his former apprenticeship to old Fezziwig. It is Christmas Eve and the festivities are about to begin.

**1** Look at how Scrooge responds to seeing old Fezziwig and his fellow apprentice, Dick Wilkins.

   **a**  What differences can you see in the way Scrooge speaks here and the way he spoke in Stave One?
   **b**  What changes in Scrooge does Dickens suggest by the way he speaks here?

Look at how Scrooge reacts to the scene with old Fezziwig:

> During the whole of this time Scrooge had acted like a man out of his wits. His heart and soul were in the scene, and with his former self. He corroborated everything, remembered everything, enjoyed everything, and underwent the strangest agitation.

Stave Two

**2** What does this suggest to you about Scrooge's thoughts and feelings?

**3** What do you think it was about this scene that made Scrooge want to say '**a word or two**' to his clerk, Bob Cratchit?

## Memories of 'his prime'

In Victorian times, an engagement to be married was regarded as a formal contract. If the engagement was broken off, the person who did so could be sued for 'breach of promise'. Women from wealthy families would have a dowry – money or property that was given to the husband when they married.

After the jolliness of old Fezziwig's ball, Scrooge is shown a sombre scene. He is older – described as '**a man in the prime of life**'. This phrase suggests that this was a time when his life should have been at its best. However, this is not the case for Scrooge. Here we see his fiancée, Belle, freeing him from his promise to marry her.

**1** Look at the description of Scrooge's face in this scene. What does it reveal?

**2** Explain what Dickens suggests through the metaphorical image of the tree.

**3** Copy and complete the following table, finding evidence to support the impressions of Belle listed in the first column.

| Impressions of Belle | Evidence |
|---|---|
| recently bereaved | she wears a 'mourning-dress' |
| upset | |
| kind | |
| unhappy in the relationship | |
| honest | |
| fair-minded | |
| perceptive | |

**4** At the end of the scene, Scrooge asks the spirit, '**Why do you delight to torture me?**'

a   What does the word '**torture**' suggest?
b   Why do you think this scene 'tortured' Scrooge?

## The final scene

The final scene is from many years later, when Marley lies close to death. Belle now lives with her husband and children. Scrooge is shown a room in her home on Christmas Eve. Dickens draws attention to the fact that it is quite small and not expensively furnished. Belle may not be wealthy, but she is clearly very happy. Dickens paints a clear picture of a loving family.

**1** When Scrooge looks at Belle's daughter with her father, his eyes grow dim at the thought that this girl might have been his own daughter and been a comfort to him in his old age. What does this suggest to you about Scrooge's thoughts and feelings at this point in the story?

**2** After Belle's husband tells her that Scrooge is all alone in the world, Scrooge asks the ghost to take him away from this place. Why do you think Scrooge '**cannot bear it**'?

> Watch the scene with Belle and Scrooge on Cambridge Elevate.

… disclosed a long, bare, melancholy room, made barer still by lines of plain deal forms and desks.

*Stave Two*

## Welfare and reclamation

The Ghost says that his 'business' is Scrooge's welfare and reclamation.

**1** What does the noun 'reclamation' suggest?

Over the course of Stave Two, we learn several important facts about the character of Scrooge:

- He was once a boy with friends and a sister who loved him, and whom he loved.
- As a youth, he was apprenticed to a generous employer and was happy in his work.
- As a young man, he won Belle's affections and, though poor, **was content to be so**'.

However, something happened to him at this point – a passion for money took root and came to overshadow his life. This ghost seeks to show Scrooge his past to make him think about his present.

**2** Copy and complete the following table to show how and why Scrooge changes in Stave Two.

| People | How Scrooge treated them | Regrets | Cause of regret |
|---|---|---|---|
| the carol singer | | | |
| Scrooge's nephew, Fred | | | |
| Scrooge's clerk, Bob Cratchit | | | |
| Scrooge's fiancée, Belle | | | |

## The power of money

The spirit calls old Fezziwig's generosity '**a small matter**' as he has not spent much money. Scrooge heatedly explains that old Fezziwig has the power to make his employers happy or unhappy, and recognises that this power is not just about money:

'Say that his power lies in words and looks; in things so slight and insignificant that it is impossible to add and count 'em up: what then? The happiness he gives is quite as great as if it cost a fortune.'

Scrooge: Stave Two

**1** Work in small groups. On a large sheet of paper, write the headings:

- Money can buy you …
- Money can't buy you …
- Can money buy you happiness?

**a** Add your own ideas about what money can and cannot buy.
**b** Think about whether money can buy you happiness. Record your opinions on the paper, giving your reasons for them.

**2** In your groups, discuss the extent to which Stave Two suggests that money cannot buy happiness.

## The meaning of the ghost's light

At the end of Stave Two, Scrooge is clearly distressed. Although he manages to press the cap down on the ghost's head, he is unable to put out the light.

**1** What does the fact that Scrooge cannot extinguish the light mean? Discuss this in pairs.

**2** The ghost's 'business' is Scrooge's welfare and his reclamation. How successful do you think he is in carrying out his business? Give reasons to support your judgement.

'The happiness he gives is quite as great as if it cost a fortune.'

*Scrooge: Stave Two*

## GETTING IT INTO WRITING

### Writing about Scrooge's feelings

When you answer questions on a novel, you should make appropriate reference to the text to support your points. There are different ways of doing this.

You can refer to the text in your own words. For example:

*Scrooge is then shown a scene from several years later. It is clear that his face has changed and not just because of age. There is something unpleasant about his appearance and his eyes seem to be constantly moving as though in search of opportunities. Dickens uses an image relating to the shadow cast by a tree to suggest that whatever has taken hold of Scrooge will follow him through life.*

You can quote directly from the text, using words and phrases in quotation marks. For example:

*Scrooge's fiancée tells him that she has been replaced by 'another idol' and that 'the master passion, Gain' has steadily replaced all his previous 'nobler aspirations'. She recognises that he is a different man from the one she fell in love with, and decides to 'release' him from their engagement.*

'Conduct me home. Why do you delight to torture me?'

*Scrooge: Stave Two*

You can use longer relevant quotations where appropriate, using a colon to introduce them. For example:

*Although upset, Belle is determined to face the truth. She knows that, given a choice, Scrooge would not now choose to marry her. She also knows that even though he might find their parting painful, it will only be for a short time: 'and you will dismiss the recollection of it gladly, as an unprofitable dream, from which it happened well that you awoke'.*

**1** Look at this question:

**How does Scrooge feel when he is shown the scene in Belle's family home?**

To answer this question well, you need to show that you:

- know what takes place in this scene
- can explain how the scene affects his feelings
- can use appropriate references and quotations to support your points.

Read this scene again. Select useful references and quotations from it and write an answer to the question.

### Learning checkpoint

**How will I know I've done this well?**

✔ highlight where you have explained how the scene affects Scrooge's feelings
✔ underline the references and quotations you have used
✔ check you have used quotation marks correctly.

### Complete this assignment on Cambridge Elevate.

## GETTING FURTHER

### Understanding allusions

An **allusion** is a reference to a person, place, thing or idea of historical, cultural or literary significance. The allusion is not explained – the reader is expected to understand the reference and its importance. While watching his younger self reading, Scrooge alludes to a range of characters:

- Ali Baba, the Sultan's Groom, the Genii, the princess, the person asleep at the gate of Damascus are all characters in *The Arabian Nights*.
- Orson and Valentine are characters in the story *The History of Valentine and Orson*.
- The parrot, Robinson Crusoe and Friday can all be found in the novel *The Life and Adventures of Robinson Crusoe*.

These were popular stories for children in the 19th century, and Dickens's readers would know these characters. Scrooge's delight in recalling them highlights his character's childlike enthusiasm and capacity for imagination.

When describing Belle's children, Dickens writes that '**unlike the celebrated herd in the poem, they were not forty children conducting themselves like one, but every child was conducting itself like forty**'. This is an allusion to the cattle described in William Wordsworth's poem 'Written in March'.

**1** Find and read the poem. What does Wordsworth note about how the cattle graze?

**2** How does knowing this reference help you understand how Belle's children are behaving?

### Read the poem 'Written in March' on Cambridge Elevate.

### Key terms

**allusion:** a reference to something that the listener or reader will recognise.

# 3

# Stave Three: The Second of the Three Spirits

## How does Dickens develop the plot and themes?

Your progress in this unit:

- explore ideas associated with light
- examine the characteristics of the Ghost of Christmas Present
- investigate the structure of Stave Three
- consider how Dickens presents the Cratchit family
- explore the significance of Ignorance and Want.

## GETTING STARTED – THE STORY AND YOU

### Ideas about light

Ideas associated with light play an important part in *A Christmas Carol*. In Stave One, Marley's Ghost laments that, in life, he did not allow the light of the '**blessed Star**' to lead him to a poor home so he could help those who lived there. In Stave Two, the Ghost of Christmas Past has a bright, clear stream of light springing from its head, which Scrooge cannot put out.

**1** Work in small groups. You are going to explore the **connotations** of the word 'light'. Write the word 'light' in the middle of a large sheet of paper. Discuss and make notes on ideas that you connect with the word. These may be:

   **a** what the word suggests to you
   **b** the significance of its use in a religious context
   **c** ideas you associate with its **antonym** – dark.

**2** In Stave One, Marley's Ghost refers to the Star of Bethlehem. In Christian tradition, this star marked the birth of Jesus and led the three Wise Men to the stable in Bethlehem where Jesus was born. Explain:

   **a** the link with this being a Christmas story
   **b** Marley's regrets.

Read the summary, then read Stave Three.

### 🔑 Key terms

**antonym:** a word with opposite meaning to another.

Scrooge pulls his curtains aside and waits for the arrival of the next spirit. As the clock strikes one, his bed becomes the centre of a very bright light. The light comes from an adjoining room, in which he finds, sitting on top of a pile of food, the Ghost of Christmas Present. Scrooge accompanies this ghost willingly – he is ready and eager to learn.

The ghost takes him through the city streets on Christmas morning. There is a cheerful atmosphere; the people, the houses and the vast range of foods are described in detail. As the bells chime, people leave to go to church or chapel. They are replaced by poorer people who are carrying their dinners to be cooked in the bakers' ovens.

The scene moves to the Cratchits' house. Scrooge sees Mrs Cratchit, the two smaller Cratchits, a boy and a girl, then Martha, the elder daughter home from service. Finally, Bob arrives carrying another son, Tiny Tim, upon his shoulder. It is a joyful scene and the family are happy, even though they are clearly poor.

After watching the Cratchits' Christmas, the ghost shows Scrooge how Christmas is celebrated widely. He takes him to a poor home where miners live, an isolated lighthouse and a ship far from the shore.

Suddenly, Scrooge finds himself in his nephew's home. He watches the family play games, even joining in himself, and begs the ghost to allow him to stay longer. They leave as the nephew toasts his Uncle Scrooge.

They now move to places of sickness and misery. Wherever they go, the spirit leaves his blessing. It seems to be growing older, and tells Scrooge that its life on earth ends at midnight. Scrooge notices something beneath the ghost's robe, which is revealed to be two wretched children, a boy named Ignorance and a girl named Want – they are Man's children. As the clock strikes 12, Scrooge lifts his eyes to see another spirit coming towards him.

## GETTING CLOSER – FOCUS ON DETAILS

### The Ghost of Christmas Present

Unlike the previous two spirits, the Ghost of Christmas Present does not come to Scrooge – it waits for him in the next room. The transformed room is described in detail before the focus shifts to the figure sitting in it. This spirit is associated with the traditions and celebrations that take place at Christmas.

**1** Work in small groups. Use the following template to record any evidence of Christmas traditions that you can find in Stave Three.

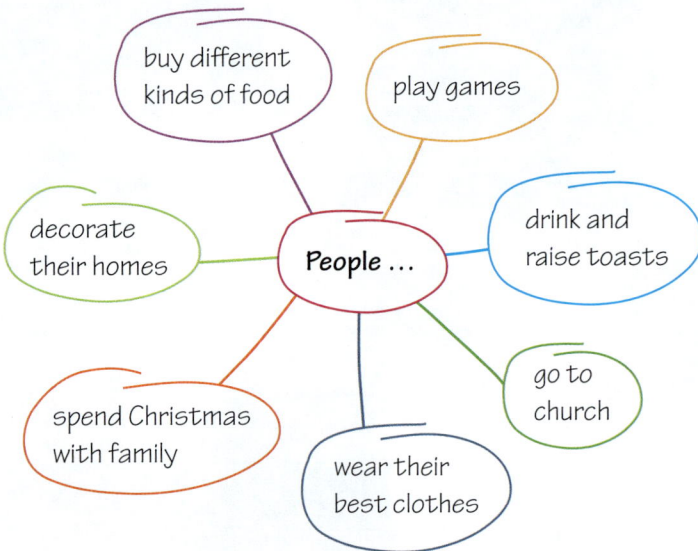

- buy different kinds of food
- play games
- decorate their homes
- People …
- drink and raise toasts
- spend Christmas with family
- go to church
- wear their best clothes

**2** Dickens lists many types of food and drink that the Victorians would have associated with Christmas. Which of these do you associate with Christmas today?

**3** Look at the description of the room where the ghost is waiting in Stave Three.

- **a** How have the walls, ceiling and fire been transformed?
- **b** What do the details of the transformed room suggest to you about the Ghost of Christmas Present?

### Early impressions of the second spirit

The Ghost of Christmas Present speaks in a commanding tone, though his eyes are '**clear and kind**'. The way that this spirit looks is significant.

**1** Using details from the text, roughly draw and annotate a sketch of the Ghost of Christmas Present. Aim to include all the details given in the description.

**2** Think about the **adjectives** underlined in the quotation below. What impression of this spirit do they help to create?

Its dark brown curls were long and <u>free</u>: free as its <u>genial</u> face, its <u>sparkling</u> eye, its <u>open</u> hand, its <u>cheery</u> voice, its <u>unconstrained</u> demeanor, and its <u>joyful</u> air.

Stave Three

**3** The ghost wears an antique scabbard or sheath – a close-fitting cover for a sword. However, this scabbard contains no sword and is eaten up with rust. What does this suggest to you about the ghost?

**4** Scrooge admits he has '**never walked forth**' with the ghost's elder brothers. What do you think he means by this? Why is it significant?

### Contexts

*A Christmas Carol* was first published in 1843. According to the Gregorian calendar – the most widely used calendar in the world today – this date signifies 1,843 years after the birth of Jesus. When the Ghost of Christmas Present says he has more than eighteen hundred brothers he is referring to the number of Christmases since the birth of Jesus.

## How the ghost teaches Scrooge

The ghost carries a glowing torch, which is compared with Plenty's horn – a **symbol** of abundance and nourishment. Throughout Stave Three, the ghost uses the torch to bless people and homes, to enrich them with the Christmas spirit. He sprinkles incense on the dinners of the poor and uses it to stop them arguing. He sprinkles Bob Cratchit's home on both arrival and departure.

Before leaving his home, Scrooge declares himself willing to learn from the ghost. He is shown several different scenes to teach him about Christmas and demonstrate how it is celebrated.

**1** Consider the three scenes listed in the table. For each scene, complete the table by:

a briefly outlining what Scrooge sees
b assessing what Scrooge might learn.

| Scene | What Scrooge sees | What Scrooge might learn |
|---|---|---|
| the streets of London on Christmas morning | | |
| Christmas in the miner's hut | | |
| Christmas evening at Fred's home | | |

Scrooge also learns through the actions and words of the spirit. He takes note of the ghost's actions and is prepared to question what he does not understand:

'Is there a peculiar flavour in what you sprinkle from your torch?' asked Scrooge.
'There is. My own.'
'Would it apply to any kind of dinner on this day?' asked Scrooge.
'To any kindly given. To a poor one most.'
'Why to a poor one most?' asked Scrooge.
'Because it needs it most.'

Stave Three

The Ghost of Christmas Present also seems prepared to challenge Scrooge directly. When Scrooge learns that Tiny Tim will die, the ghost throws his own words from Stave One back at him: **'What then? If he be like to die, he had better do it and decrease the surplus population.'** When the ghost sees that Scrooge regrets his words, he does not comfort him, but instead emphasises his message.

**2** Write a short paragraph explaining how Dickens gives force to the ghost's argument. Include reference to:

a   how the adjective **'adamant'** is used
b   the effect of the phrase **'wicked cant'**
c   the question
d   the image of the insect on the leaf
e   anything else you think relevant.

> **Watch the conflict between Scrooge and the ghost on Cambridge Elevate.**

## PUTTING DETAILS TO USE

### The structure of Stave Three

Writers choose to develop their ideas in a particular sequence. Their choices affect the order:

- of ideas in a complete story
- of ideas in a chapter
- of ideas in a paragraph
- of words and ideas in a sentence.

In *A Christmas Carol*, the reader is transported through time. Stave One starts seven years before the present, with the death of Marley, then moves to Christmas Eve in the present. Stave Two covers many years of Scrooge's past life, but starts and ends in the present. Stave Three covers a single day – Christmas Day – and draws on and develops events and ideas from the first two staves. For example in Stave One, Scrooge treats his clerk meanly. In Stave Two, having witnessed old Fezziwig's generosity, Scrooge wishes he could speak with Cratchit. In Stave Three, he sees the

Cratchit family at home and is directly confronted with their poverty – something he has the power to change.

Stave Three is the middle stave; it is also the longest. The events are narrated in chronological order – the order in which they occur.

**1** Put the following events in the order they appear in the stave:

a   The ghost sprinkles the dinners of the poor.
b   They visit the miners living on a bleak moor.
c   The ghost reveals Want and Ignorance just before midnight.
d   Martha Cratchit arrives home in time for Christmas dinner.
e   The ghost introduces himself.
f   Lighthouse keepers and sailors remember Christmas.
g   They wander through the city streets on Christmas morning.
h   Scrooge joins in the games at his nephew's on Christmas evening.
i   The ghost foretells the death of Tiny Tim.
j   The ghost clearly grows older.

### The passage of time

At the start of Stave Three, the **'bell struck once'**. It is 1 a.m. at the start of Christmas Day morning. The stave closes with the bell striking midnight at the end of Christmas Day. Throughout the stave, Dickens makes sure his reader is aware that time is passing and the day is moving on. He does this through the chronological sequencing of events: the main scenes relate to Christmas morning on the streets of London, Christmas dinner at the Cratchit house, Christmas evening at Fred's, and the revelation of Want and Ignorance just before midnight. He also uses language to effectively convey the passing of time.

> **Find out more about plot and structure in** *A Christmas Carol* **in Unit 6.**

Dickens creates a clear visual image of the sun setting:

Down in the west the setting sun had left <u>a streak of fiery red</u>, which <u>glared upon the desolation</u> for an instant, <u>like a sullen eye, and frowning</u>, <u>lower, lower yet</u>, was <u>lost in the thick gloom of darkest night</u>.

*Stave Three*

**1** What effect do the underlined words have in this extract? Record your ideas in a table like this.

| Underlined words | Effects |
|---|---|
| 'a streak of fiery red' | This **noun phrase** could suggest a sense of the disappearing sun – only a 'streak' remains. It is 'fiery red', these adjectives perhaps suggesting anger at leaving the day, Christmas Day, behind. |
| 'glared upon the desolation' | The verb 'glared' might represent … |

**Key terms**

**noun phrase:** a group of words that function as a noun.

Down in the west the setting sun had left a streak of fiery red, which glared upon the desolation for an instant …

*Stave Three*

## Paragraph structure

Dickens varies the length of his paragraphs. Sometimes he uses short paragraphs to create a particular effect. For example he writes three developed paragraphs to describe Scrooge waking up and waiting for the ghost. He then writes this short paragraph to create tension and mystery:

> The moment Scrooge's hand was on the lock, a strange voice called him by his name, and bade him enter. He obeyed.

Stave Three

Notice how:

- the owner of the voice knows immediately that Scrooge is there
- Scrooge does not know the voice, yet its owner knows him
- the voice carries authority
- Scrooge's submission is emphasised.

Sometimes Dickens **juxtaposes** viewpoints within a paragraph to emphasise differences between them. The order in which he presents the perspectives is often significant.

**1** Read again the paragraph that describes the Cratchits at the point where Scrooge and the Ghost of Christmas Present are about to leave. It contains three sentences. Identify which sentence:

- **a** views the Cratchits in terms of their poverty and few possessions
- **b** states that there was nothing remarkable about the Cratchits
- **c** views the Cratchits in terms of their feelings and relationships
- **d** explains why there was nothing remarkable about the Cratchits
- **e** starts with 'but' to mark a change of direction
- **f** emphasises the happiness of the Cratchits.

### Learning checkpoint

As well as examining the ways ideas are ordered within a paragraph, you need to think about the **links** Dickens makes between paragraphs.

Read the two paragraphs about the lighthouse and its keepers. Examine:

✔ the focus of each paragraph
✔ the contrast between the paragraphs
✔ the effect of the word 'but' at the start of the second paragraph
✔ how the description of the elder lighthouse keeper reflects the weather described in the first paragraph.

The Ghost of Christmas Present carries a glowing torch. What symbolic significance might the lighthouse have?

## Christmas at the Cratchits

The Cratchits' Christmas is central to Stave Three. The family is poor: Bob Cratchit earns very little and the family wear old and often-mended clothes. However, they do not complain – they are happy and grateful for what they have.

**Dialogue** is an important feature of narrative. It allows the reader to hear the characters directly and make judgements on them.

**1** Look at the part of the scene where Bob Cratchit toasts Scrooge. How does Dickens use dialogue to show the reader:

  **a** Mrs Cratchit's feelings
  **b** the different temperaments of Bob and his wife
  **c** the relationship between Bob and his wife?

## Christmas dinner

Dinner is the focal point of the Cratchit Christmas. Once the family is assembled and the goose has been fetched, there is a great deal of activity.

**1** Find a section where Dickens describes the family's Christmas dinner celebrations. How does Dickens use language to:

  **a** create the idea of a busy Christmas Day?
  **b** show the reader that this is a united family that works together?

**2** Look at the extract. Explain how Dickens:

  **a** creates a sense of drama
  **b** reinforces the image of a family.

It was succeeded by a breathless pause, as Mrs. Cratchit, looking slowly all along the carving-knife, prepared to plunge it in the breast; but when she did, and when the long expected gush of stuffing issued forth, one murmur of delight arose all round the board …

Stave Three

**3** Read the paragraph beginning '**Oh, a wonderful pudding!**' What do you think is the purpose of this paragraph? Why do you think this? Consider the following:

  **a** responses to the pudding
  **b** use of vocabulary
  **c** use of varied sentence structures.

## Family

Family is a recurring idea in *A Christmas Carol*. In Stave Two, we learn that Scrooge:

- was kept from his family at Christmas as a child
- watches Belle's family scene with regret
- realises that had he taken a different course, he too could have had a daughter to care for him in his old age.

**1** In Stave Three, Scrooge is moved by the Cratchit family scene. Consider everything you have learnt about the Cratchit family. Find evidence to support each of the following statements. This might be detail or quotations.

  **a** The family are poor.
  **b** The father and mother have traditional roles in the family.
  **c** Both parents work hard.
  **d** The family are supportive of one another.
  **e** The family work together.

**2** Money may not be needed for happiness, but it is shown to be necessary for health. How does Dickens show, through the character of Tiny Tim, that it is needed for health?

**Watch a video about the two family scenes on Cambridge Elevate.**

**Key terms**

**juxtapose:** to place two ideas or things near each other to invite comparison or contrast.
**dialogue:** a conversation between two or more people in a piece of writing.

### Ignorance and Want

After showing Scrooge how Christmas is a time of widespread celebration and happiness, the Ghost of Christmas Present shows Scrooge two children it is sheltering under its robes. Before explaining who these children are, Dickens describes them. He uses two lists, each containing five adjectives:

| First list | Second list |
| --- | --- |
| wretched | yellow |
| abject | meagre |
| frightful | ragged |
| hideous | scowling |
| miserable | wolfish |

**1** Which adjectives suggest that these children:

   **a** are to be pitied
   **b** are to be feared?

**2** What are the connotations of the word 'wolfish'? What does this adjective suggest about the children?

### Language to express ideas

The children Ignorance and Want shatter the readers' expectations of what children might and should look like. However, they do have some childlike qualities. In two carefully balanced sentences, Dickens shows us both the children's potential and the reality of their existence.

| The potential | The reality |
| --- | --- |
| 'Where graceful youth should have filled their features out, and touched them with its freshest tints, | a stale and shrivelled hand, like that of age, had pinched, and twisted them, and pulled them into shreds.' |
| 'Where angels might have sat enthroned, | devils lurked, and glared out menacing.' |

**1** How does Dickens use language in these sentences to show the **contrast** between the children's potential and reality of their existence? Think about Dickens's use of:

   **a** nouns (words that refer to people, places, things and ideas)
   **b** adjectives (words used to enhance the meaning of nouns)
   **c** verbs (words that convey actions, thoughts and feelings)
   **d** **adverbs** (words used to enhance the meaning of verbs).

> **Key terms**
>
> **contrast:** the way in which two or more things are different from one another.
>
> **adverb:** a word that adds to the meaning of a verb, adjective or other adverb.

… back came Tiny Tim before another word was spoken, escorted by his brother and sister to his stool by the fire …

*Stave Three*

The Ghost of Christmas Present tells Scrooge that the children are Man's and that they cling to him, '**appealing from their fathers**'. Children usually ask their fathers for help, yet these children appeal 'from' not 'to' their fathers. The spirit makes clear to Scrooge that Mankind is responsible for all its children and that he, Scrooge, shares that responsibility.

In portraying Ignorance and Want as children, Dickens is using a language technique called **personification** – giving ideas a human form. This personification presents the reader with a visual image of the damage created by 'ignorance' and 'want'.

**2** The following statements offer some ideas about the possible significance of the children Ignorance and Want. Give each statement a number from 1 to 5 to indicate how far you agree with them, where 1 is strongly agree and 5 is disagree.

   **a**   Poverty and lack of education begin in childhood.
   **b**   Ignorance is more dangerous than poverty.
   **c**   If the poor are not educated, they have no chance to escape the cycle of poverty.
   **d**   Children who live in poverty are hidden from most people's eyes and rarely thought of.
   **e**   The two children depict the hidden ugliness of Victorian society.
   **f**   Children are the responsibility of society.
   **g**   It is adults who destroy the innocence of childhood.
   **h**   Everyone will suffer if the poor are not properly cared for.
   **i**   The reader is reminded that Scrooge is also guilty of ignorance.
   **j**   People have a duty to help the poor whenever the opportunity arises.

**3** With genuine concern, Scrooge asks of the children: '**Have they no refuge or resources?**' Remind yourself of Scrooge's conversation with the two portly gentlemen in Stave One. Then write a short paragraph explaining the significance of the ghost's reply to Scrooge's question.

The ghost's manner changes as he tells Scrooge that he should '**most of all beware this boy, for on his brow I see that written which is Doom**'. He loses his jolly tone and becomes angry.

**4** What does the ghost say? Who do you think this message is addressed to and why?

---

**Key terms**

**personification:** a type of metaphor that gives human qualities to inanimate objects.

'… beware of this boy, for on his brow I see that written which is Doom.'

*Ghost of Christmas Present: Stave Three*

## GETTING IT INTO WRITING

### Writing about Ignorance and Want

Read this sample student response to the following question:

**How does Dickens present Tiny Tim in Stave Three?**

Tiny Tim is Bob Cratchit's son and when we first meet him we are told he had 'his limbs supported by an iron frame'. He had just been to church where he hoped the people would see him because it would make them remember 'who made lame beggars walk and blind men see'.

> This student describes and uses quotation.

Now look at another response, in which a student develops a range of comments.

In Stave Three, Dickens perhaps suggests that Tiny Tim is a child with a sickly body but a strong spirit. Dickens describes how he has a 'little' crutch, a 'withered, little hand' and a 'plaintive little voice'. Dickens's use of adjectives emphasises his frailty, convincing readers of the ghost's prediction that he will die soon if his future remains 'unaltered'. Even so, Dickens's description of 'his happy crutch' and the way he rides home from church on his father's shoulders after being hustled away by his brothers seems to suggest that he moves speedily. Dickens cleverly reflects this combination of physical weakness and strong spirit with the juxtaposition of adverb and verb use in 'He feebly cried Hurrah!', with the final exclamation perhaps suggesting a sense of triumph over adversity.

**1** What do you think is good about this response? Why? Write down some annotations pointing out where the student has shown particular skills.

The following questions can help you write detailed and informative comments about parts of a text:

- **Infer:** What does this suggest or imply?
- **Explore:** Why has the writer done this?
- **Analyse:** How does the writer use language to create a picture and/or influence the reader?

Think about this task:

**How does Dickens present the children, Ignorance and Want, in Stave Three?**

Look at the following responses and the annotations.

The reader learns that they are 'wolfish' in appearance but also that they are 'prostrate in their humility'.

> Infer: What different ideas about the children are suggested by these quotations?

The children are the last thing the Spirit shows to Scrooge.

> Explore: Why do you think the spirit keeps the children until last?

Dickens uses a balanced sentence when writing about the children: 'Where angels might have sat enthroned, devils lurked, and glared out menacing.'

> Analyse: How does Dickens use sentence structure and word choice to emphasise a contrast?

2 Use the questions at the end of each response to develop a more detailed comment.

3 Compare your developed comments with a partner. Suggest improvements if you can.

✔ **Complete this assignment on Cambridge Elevate.**

## GETTING FURTHER

### More about Tiny Tim

The reader is not told what is wrong with Tiny Tim, only that he:

- is very little and uses a crutch
- has his limbs supported by an iron frame
- has a withered hand
- will soon die if not helped.

It was not uncommon in Victorian England for children to die while they were young. It was once estimated that one-third of all deaths in a year in London were those of children. While child mortality was highest in poor families, better-off ones were also affected. Dickens's own daughter, Dora, died when she was nine months old.

1 Use the internet to find out more about child mortality in Victorian England. How do you think this might have affected Dickens's portrayal of poverty in *A Christmas Carol*?

'Spirit,' said Scrooge, with an interest he had never felt before, 'tell me if Tiny Tim will live.'

*Stave Three*

# 4

## Stave Four: The Last of the Spirits

### How does Dickens build to the climax?

Your progress in this unit:
- examine how Dickens creates an image of the phantom
- learn about the City
- explore ideas connected with death
- consider the dramatic qualities of the ghosts.

## GETTING STARTED – THE STORY AND YOU

### A phantom of darkness

The Ghost of Christmas Yet to Come first makes an appearance at the end of Stave Three, just after the disappearance of the Ghost of Christmas Present. It is described as '**a solemn Phantom, draped and hooded, coming, like a mist along the ground**' towards Scrooge. Already the reader senses that this is the most serious, and the most mysterious, of Scrooge's visitors. This ghost seems shrouded in darkness.

Dickens creates a clear impression of the Ghost of Christmas Yet to Come right from the start of Stave Four, saying '**The Phantom slowly, gravely, silently approached**' and that it '**seemed to scatter gloom and mystery**'.

**1** Find other quotations in Stave Four that describe the Ghost of Christmas Yet to Come. Choose quotations that describe how the ghost moves, how it looks and its effect on Scrooge.

Read the summary, then read Stave Four.

## GETTING CLOSER – FOCUS ON DETAILS

### The Ghost of Christmas Yet to Come

**1** In 'Getting it into writing' in Unit 3, you learnt that you need to develop your comments to show that you can explore ideas and analyse use of language. Now develop a response to this question:

**How does Dickens present the Ghost of Christmas Yet to Come in the opening paragraphs of Stave Four?**

**2** Annotate your response to show where you have:

**a** explored ideas
**b** analysed the use of language.

# STAVE FOUR: THE LAST OF THE SPIRITS

Scrooge says he fears the Ghost of Christmas Yet to Come more than any of the others. However, he follows it willingly and hopes it will help him live a different life in the future. They enter the City and hear a group of merchants discussing someone's death. Next they overhear two businessmen talking and they also refer to a death.

From there, the ghost and Scrooge move to a shop run by a man called Joe. It is in a part of town where Scrooge had never been before. A charwoman, laundress and undertaker's man enter with goods they hope to sell to Joe. The goods have been stolen from a dead man. They include the curtains and blankets from the dead man's bed, and even the shirt he was to be buried in. Scrooge is appalled by their behaviour.

The scene suddenly changes and the ghost and Scrooge are in a bedroom. A body is on the bed but Scrooge is unable to move the cover to look at it. He reflects on the life this man must have led to bring him to this lonely end.

Scrooge asks the ghost to show him anyone who feels emotion at this man's death and is shown a mother with her children, waiting for her husband to return. When he does, she is thankful for the news that the merciless man to whom they owe money has died.

Scrooge asks the ghost to show him some tenderness connected with death and he is taken to Bob Cratchit's home, where the family are grief-stricken at the death of Tiny Tim.

From there the spirit takes Scrooge to a churchyard and points to a neglected grave, which bears the name Ebenezer Scrooge. Scrooge begs to be given the chance to change his future. The phantom collapses and turns into a bedpost.

51

**3** Think about the relationship between the ghost and Scrooge in this stave. Make notes on:

  **a** what the ghost shows Scrooge
  **b** how Scrooge responds to the ghost
  **c** how the ghost responds to Scrooge.

**4** The '**spectral hand**' is all that Scrooge can see of the ghost, which uses its hand and finger to point the way.

  **a** Find and make a note of all the references to the phantom's hand or its finger.
  **b** What changes have taken place with the hand by the end of Stave Four? What do you think these changes indicate?

## The City

Dickens uses a range of techniques to describe the City and the people who work there. For example:

---

They scarcely seemed to enter the city; for the city rather seemed to spring up about them, and encompass them of its own act. But there they were in the heart of it.

*Stave Four*

---

**1** What are the effects of the following language techniques in this extract?

  **a** **Personification** ('**encompasses them of its own act**').
  **b** **Metaphor** ('**they were in the heart of it**').

**2** How does the choice of verbs and **adjectives** in the following extract help to create an impression of the merchants?

---

… who hurried up and down, and chinked the money in their pockets, and conversed in groups, and looked at their watches, and trifled thoughtfully with their great gold seals.

*Stave Four*

---

**▶ Watch a video about London in the 19th century on Cambridge Elevate.**

### ℹ Contexts

When writing about the City, Dickens is referring to London's business and financial centre, a place frequented by merchants and businessmen. At its heart lies the London Stock Exchange. In 1802, the Stock Exchange moved into a new building in Capel Court – possibly the same court that Scrooge refers to when speaking of '**his place of occupation**'. As a man of business, Scrooge would have known this area well. In *A Christmas Carol*, the Exchange is referred to as ''Change, which is a common abbreviation used at that time. It is to the City that the Ghost of Christmas Yet to Come first takes Scrooge.

**3** Look at Dickens's physical descriptions of the businessmen. What impression of these men do Dickens's word choices and use of **simile** give the reader?

### ⇄ Find out more about language in *A Christmas Carol* in Unit 10.

### Clues in the text

In this part of the story, Dickens uses **dramatic irony** – giving the reader clues to help them understand what Scrooge does not. Overhearing the conversation between the businessmen, the reader begins to suspect that the dead man is Scrooge, but Scrooge himself does not yet realise this.

**1** Identify the clues that Dickens gives in this passage to help the reader understand that the dead man is Scrooge. They may be to do with:

  **a** what is said about the dead man
  **b** the attitudes of the businessmen towards the dead man.

### 🔑 Key terms

**dramatic irony:** when the reader or audience knows something that a character in a novel or play does not.

# The hand was pointed straight before them.

*Stave Four*

## PUTTING DETAILS TO USE

### The other side of the City

In 1850, seven years after the publication of *A Christmas Carol*, Dickens described an area of Westminster that he called 'The Devil's Acre'. He wanted to draw his readers' attention to what lay behind the external beauty of Westminster:

The most lordly streets are frequently but a mask for the squalid district which lies behind them. [...] The district, which is small in area, is one of the most populous in London, almost every house being crowded with numerous families, and multitudes of lodgers. There are other parts of the town as filthy, dingy, and forbidding in appearance as this. [...] But there are none in which guilt of all kinds and degrees converges in such volume as on this, the moral plague-spot not only of the metropolis, but also of the kingdom.

Dickens seems to have had this area in mind when describing this side of the City in Stave Four:

The ways were foul and narrow; the shops and houses wretched; the people half-naked, drunken, slipshod, ugly. Alleys and archways, like so many cesspools, disgorged their offences of smell, and dirt, and life, upon the straggling streets; and the whole quarter reeked with crime, with filth, and misery.

Stave Four

**1** Make a list of the adjectives, verbs and nouns Dickens uses in this passage. Then re-read the passage and answer the following question:

**What do you think Dickens is suggesting about this area of London, and how did it make you feel when you read it?**

**2** Now write a developed paragraph explaining how Dickens uses language to create an image of this part of the City. Remember to:

a refer directly to words and phrases
b comment on their effects
c use correct terminology when describing language features.

## The thieves

To illustrate the nature of the people who frequent this place, Dickens introduces the **characters** of the charwoman, laundress and undertaker's man. They bring their stolen goods to sell to Joe, the owner of the shop. Unusually, there is little direct description of any of these four characters. It is as though their actions and words reveal all that needs to be known about them.

**1** Think about the order in which the stolen goods are revealed. Suggest why Dickens might have chosen this order.

Scrooge is appalled by these people and what they have done. He '**viewed them with a detestation and disgust which could hardly have been greater**'. The reader may share his feelings, but it is clear that there is irony in the fact that the thieves view Scrooge with equal distaste. He considers them to be villains; they hold the same opinion of him.

**2** Look at how each of the thieves talks about Scrooge. In pairs, talk about how these descriptions:

   **a** illustrate the belief that Scrooge got what he deserved
   **b** echo Marley's Ghost's words when he says his chain was '**forged in life**'
   **c** reflect the description of Scrooge as being '**solitary as an oyster**' in Stave One
   **d** suggest that, in some ways, the thieves are like Scrooge.

### Learning checkpoint

Joe is the shopkeeper who receives the stolen goods from the charwoman, the laundress and the undertaker's man. Read the paragraph that describes his shop, starting with '**Far in this den of infamous resort, there was a low-browed, beetling shop**'.

**1** The paragraph contains four sentences. Identify the subject of each sentence.

**2** How does Dickens structure the paragraph and use language to create a picture of the shop and the shopkeeper? Think about:

   **a** how the paragraph starts and ends
   **b** the subject and order of the sentences
   **c** Dickens's use of lists
   **d** Dickens's use of adjectives.

Watch a video about Joe's shop on Cambridge Elevate.

## The theme of death

The Ghost of Christmas Yet to Come takes Scrooge to the bedchamber of the dead man. The reader, of course, knows that this is Scrooge, though Scrooge himself appears not to realise this even now.

**1** Dickens conveys the horror of the corpse through suggestion rather than direct description:

---

… beneath a ragged sheet, there lay a something covered up, which, though it was dumb, announced itself in awful language.

---

Stave Four

   **a** What does the unusual phrase '**a something**' suggest?
   **b** What does the verb '**announced**' suggest?
   **c** What is the effect of the adjective '**awful**'?

**2** What does Dickens suggest or imply, without clearly stating, in the following extract?

---

A cat was tearing at the door, and there was a sound of gnawing rats beneath the hearth-stone. What *they* wanted in the room of death, and why they were so restless and disturbed, Scrooge did not dare to think.

---

Stave Four

Scrooge wants to lift the cover from the man's face, but he cannot do so. He does, however, realise that factors about this man have brought about his sad end – his greed, his cruelty to others and his lack of joy in life. In this part of the story, the **narrator** reflects on the power of death. He makes a number of points that can help us to understand Dickens's perspective on this **theme**.

**3** Match the extract to its likely explanation.

| Extract | Explanation |
|---|---|
| 'Oh, cold, cold, rigid, dreadful Death, set up thine altar here […] for this is thy dominion!' | What matters is not that the person is dead now, but what they achieved in their lifetime. |
| 'But of the loved, revered, and honoured head thou canst not […] one feature odious.' | It is people like this dead man that Death has power over. |
| 'It is not that the hand is heavy […] the heart brave, warm, and tender; and the pulse a man's.' | A person's good deeds in life will stay with the world forever. |
| 'Strike, Shadow, strike. And see his good deeds springing from the wound, to sow the world with life immortal!' | Death cannot diminish those who are loved. |

## The death of Tiny Tim

In the first scene of death, Dickens shows us a man '**unwatched, unwept, uncared for**'. Death has power over him because he was unloved. When Scrooge asks the ghost to let him see a softer side to death, it takes him to the home of Bob Cratchit, where Tiny Tim has died. This scene presents a marked **contrast** with the one before.

**1** Make a note of evidence or quotations from this scene that could be used to show the family's:

    **a**    grief for the loss of Tiny Tim
    **b**    acceptance of his death
    **c**    acknowledgement of the effect he had on their lives
    **d**    concern and support for one another.

Bob Cratchit has been that day to arrange Tiny Tim's funeral and burial place. Immediately following this scene, the ghost takes Scrooge to his own burial place.

It was a worthy place. Walled in by houses; overrun by grass and weeds, the growth of vegetation's death, no life; choked up with too much burying; fat with repleted appetite.

Stave Four

**2** The contrast between the two burial places is clear. Dickens uses the term '**worthy place**' ironically. What do you think he actually means? What does his description suggest about this graveyard?

## The ghosts

There are four ghosts in *A Christmas Carol*. Marley's Ghost is the only one of these that is the spirit of a dead person. The others are spirits of Christmas, representing the past, the present and the future.

**1** Copy and complete the following table to gather detail about these ghosts and show the effect each one has on Scrooge.

|  | Marley's Ghost | The Ghost of Christmas Past | The Ghost of Christmas Present | The Ghost of Christmas Yet to Come |
|---|---|---|---|---|
| what it looks like |  |  |  |  |
| main characteristics |  |  |  |  |
| what it shows Scrooge |  |  |  |  |
| attitude towards Scrooge |  |  |  |  |
| what Scrooge learns from it |  |  |  |  |

… overrun by grass and weeds, the growth of vegetation's death, no life; choked up with too much burying …

*Stave Four*

## Presenting the ghosts

Less than two months after the publication of *A Christmas Carol*, there were at least eight theatrical versions of it in production. Since then, there have been hundreds more adaptations for stage, radio, television and film. Clearly, the ghosts have a dramatic quality that works well on stage and screen.

**1** If you had to present each of the ghosts in a stage or screen version of *A Christmas Carol*, how would you do it? Would you use:

    **a**   illuminated skeletons
    **b**   spot-lit figures dressed in white robes
    **c**   voices only
    **d**   figures appearing exactly as described by Dickens
    **e**   something else?

**2** Consider the first appearance of each ghost. How would you present this to have a dramatic impact on your viewers?

## GETTING IT INTO WRITING

### Writing about the City

When you write an essay in response to a question, you should first plan your answer. Planning will ensure that you:

- answer the question set
- cover the relevant points in a logical order
- make appropriate reference to the text.

Look at the following question:

**How does Dickens present the death of Tiny Tim in Stave Four?**

**1** Start by thinking about the things you could write in answer to this question. Use the prompts to help you develop your ideas. Make a note of any quotations you could use in your response.

    **a**   What do you learn directly and indirectly about the family's response to his death? How does Dickens use language to convey feelings?
    **b**   How might Dickens want his readers to respond to this death?
    **c**   Where does Dickens position this death in Stave Four?
    **d**   What is suggested or implied about the significance of Tiny Tim's death?

Once you have gathered ideas and quotations, you need to decide how to group them and the order in which you will write about them.

**2** Identify four or five sections in Stave Four that you would write about in your essay. Find quotations you would select to support your ideas. Share your choices with a partner.

**3** Now generate ideas and quotations you could use in response to the following question:

**How does Dickens present the City in Stave Four?**

Start by thinking about:

- what you learn about the City
- the methods Dickens uses to present the City
- the contrasts within the City
- what is revealed about Scrooge through Dickens's portrayal of the City.

**4** Decide and make notes on a possible order for your answer.

**5** Compare your ideas with a partner's. Make improvements if you need to.

✔ **Complete this assignment on Cambridge Elevate.**

## GETTING FURTHER

### The context of Dickens's childhood

In 1824, when Dickens had just turned 12, his father was arrested for debt and sent to Marshalsea prison, where he remained for two months. It was a difficult time for Dickens – he had to pawn the family's furniture and books and he was forced to take a job at Warren's factory, covering and labelling pots of shoe blacking (polish). Separated from his family during the week, it was a time of great loneliness and personal pain for Dickens – and one that he never forgot.

**1** Re-read the scene that immediately follows Scrooge's request that the Ghost of Christmas Yet to Come show him any '**person in the town who feels emotion caused by this man's death**'. In what ways does this scene suggest that Dickens understood and empathised with those in debt?

# 5

## Stave Five: The End of It

How does Dickens bring about a happy ending?

Your progress in this unit:
- review Dickens's use of children in *A Christmas Carol*
- understand how Scrooge keeps his promises
- examine how Dickens creates a joyful tone
- explore why *A Christmas Carol* is still popular today.

## GETTING STARTED – THE STORY AND YOU

### The role of children in *A Christmas Carol*

Children play an important part in *A Christmas Carol*. We learn about Scrooge's own childhood and are shown children in family scenes in the homes of Belle, Bob Cratchit, the miners and the couple who owed Scrooge money. Finally, in the figures of Ignorance and Want, we are shown children whose lives have been ruined by a lack of education and the simple necessities of life.

**1** Look at the **adjectives** in the word bank. Which of these do you associate with children?

| | | |
|---|---|---|
| innocent | wicked | energetic |
| vulnerable | natural | pure |
| needy | trustful | open |
| cute | naive | guileless |
| devious | simple | loving |
| mischievous | defenceless | affectionate |
| naughty | playful | evil |

**2** Children had just as much emotional appeal in Victorian times as they do today. In pairs, discuss why you think Dickens makes such extensive use of children in *A Christmas Carol*.

**Find out more about the importance of children in *A Christmas Carol* on Cambridge Elevate.**

Read the summary, then read Stave Five.

## GETTING CLOSER – FOCUS ON DETAILS

### Scrooge keeps his promises

At the start of Stave Five, Scrooge awakens, filled with joy.

**1** How does Dickens show Scrooge to be childlike and playful in his actions and in his words?

At the end of Stave Four, Scrooge promises **'I will live in the Past, the Present, and the Future. The Spirits of all Three shall strive within me.'** It is these words that finally make the Ghost of Christmas Yet to Come relent. In Stave Five, on realising that he is still alive, Scrooge repeats these promises. The reader sees Scrooge being true to his word as he takes direct action based on the things he has learnt.

Scrooge does not fall asleep after the Ghost of Christmas Yet to Come turns into a bedpost. He is awake and excited that he is still alive and takes delight in seeing that his bed curtains have not been torn down and that the saucepan with its gruel is still there. He notes the door through which Marley's Ghost entered and does not doubt his meetings with the spirits.

The bells ring and he asks a passing boy what day it is. In surprise, the boy replies that it is Christmas Day. Delighted to discover that he has not missed it, Scrooge sends the boy to fetch the big prize turkey from the butcher, and promises him a generous reward for speedy service. When it arrives, he pays for a cab for it to be taken to Bob Cratchit's house.

Once shaved and dressed, Scrooge ventures into the streets and smiles at everyone he passes. He meets one of the portly gentlemen who visited him in Stave One and promises a large sum of money to charity. He then goes to church and in the afternoon he visits his nephew's home, where he is warmly welcomed.

The following morning, Scrooge is at his office early. When Bob Cratchit arrives late, he tricks him into thinking he is angry with him and then surprises him by promising him a pay rise and help with his family.

At the end of the story, the narrator assures the reader that Tiny Tim did not die and that Scrooge kept his word and became a good man. Some people laughed at the change in Scrooge but he was not bothered by this. He never saw the spirits again but he always kept Christmas well. The stave, and the story, ends with Tiny Tim's words '**God bless us, every one!**'

**2** Complete the following table to show how Scrooge's actions reveal what he has learnt from his ghostly experiences.

| Scrooge's actions | What Scrooge has learnt | When/how Scrooge learnt it |
|---|---|---|
| Scrooge sends a large turkey to the Cratchit home and promises to raise Bob's salary. | That a good employer should treat his employees well and that Bob and his family are deserving of better treatment. | When he relives old Fezziwig's ball (Stave Two) and when he watches the family at Christmas dinner (Stave Three). |
| Scrooge makes a large donation to charity. | | |
| Scrooge joins his nephew at home for Christmas. | | |
| Scrooge becomes a 'second father' to Tiny Tim. | | |

↔ **Find out more about character and characterisation in *A Christmas Carol* in Unit 8.**

## The meaning of 'honouring' Christmas

At the end of Stave Four, Scrooge also says that he will honour Christmas **'in his heart'** and **'try to keep it all the year'**.

**1** What message do you think Dickens was giving with these words? What do they suggest Christmas is really about?

**2** In Stave Five, nothing around Scrooge has changed – but his attitude has. Track these changes by answering the questions in the second column of the following table.

| Stave One | Stave Five |
|---|---|
| Scrooge thinks that 'every idiot who goes about with "Merry Christmas" on his lips should be boiled with his own pudding, and buried with a stake of holly through his heart.' | How does he feel about the words 'Merry Christmas'? |
| When the carol singer calls he seizes his ruler to frighten him off. | How does he respond to the boy who fetches the turkey? |
| Scrooge 'growls' and 'mutters' and often says 'Humbug'. He was 'not much in the habit of cracking jokes'. | What references can you find to Scrooge's laughter? |
| Scrooge is described as 'solitary as an oyster'. He liked to 'edge his way along the crowded paths of life, warning all human sympathy to keep its distance'. | What evidence can you find to suggest that Scrooge now enjoys the company of other people? |

🎥 **Watch a video of Scrooge finding out it is Christmas Day on Cambridge Elevate.**

## PUTTING DETAILS TO USE

### How Dickens creates a sense of joy

The word **tone** is often used to describe the mood or attitude the writer conveys in a piece of writing. The tone of Stave Four is very dark. It is filled with a sense of dread and impending doom as Scrooge gradually realises his fate if he does not change his ways. The tone of Stave Five is very different.

**1** Write down three adjectives you would use to describe the tone of Stave Five.

Dickens creates and sustains this tone through:

- the ways he presents Scrooge's speech, thoughts and feelings
- comments made by the **narrator**
- use of punctuation.

Scrooge's speech shows the change in him and conveys his excitement and joy:

'I am as light as a feather, I am as happy as an angel, I am as merry as a school-boy. I am as giddy as a drunken man. A merry Christmas to everybody! A Happy New Year to all the world! Hallo here! Whoop! Hallo!'

*Scrooge: Stave Five*

**2** Copy the quotation. Annotate it to show how Dickens uses Scrooge's spoken words to reveal his feelings.

'I am as light as a feather, I am as happy as an angel, I am as merry as a school-boy.'

*Scrooge: Stave Five*

## Scrooge's thoughts and feelings

Through the narrator, Dickens **shows** rather than **tells** the reader what Scrooge is thinking and feeling:

> Suggests the powerful emotions Scrooge feels.

He was checked in his transports by the churches ringing out the lustiest peals he had ever heard. Clash, clang, hammer, ding, dong, bell. Bell, dong, ding, hammer, clang, clash! Oh, glorious, glorious!

Stave Five

> Suggests the bells are full of life and energy.

> Scrooge is hearing the bells as though for the first time.

**1** Do you agree with the interpretation of this extract in the annotations? Why, or why not?

**2** What other language devices does Dickens use in this extract? What effect do they have?

**3** Dickens uses **onomatopoeic** words to convey the sounds of the bells. Read this list aloud. What effect do these words have?

**4** Find another short extract from the start of Stave Five. Annotate it to show how Dickens uses the narrator's words to suggest Scrooge's thoughts and feelings.

> Find out more about language in *A Christmas Carol* in Unit 10.

## The narrator's commentary

Throughout Stave Five, the narrator gives a commentary on Scrooge's new attitude to life and how he shows this in his behaviour. These comments help sustain the joyful tone. For example when Scrooge first laughs out loud, the narrator comments: '**Really for a man who had been out of practice for so many years, it was a splendid laugh, a most illustrious laugh. The father of a long, long line of brilliant laughs!**'

**1** What do the words '**splendid**' and '**illustrious**' suggest?

**2** What does the second sentence hint at?

**3** Find the following quotations in the text. For each one, explain how Dickens uses the narrator's comment to add good humour to the text.

a **The boy was off like a shot. He must have had a steady hand at a trigger who could have got a shot off half so fast.**

b **It was a turkey! He never could have stood upon his legs, that bird. He would have snapped 'em short off in a minute, like sticks of sealing-wax.**

c **The chuckle with which he said this, and the chuckle with which he paid for the turkey […] were only to be exceeded by the chuckle with which he sat down breathless in his chair again, and chuckled till he cried.**

### Key terms

**onomatopoeic:** describing a word whose sound suggests its meaning.

Clash, clang, hammer,
ding, dong, bell. Bell,
dong, ding, hammer,
clang, clash!

*Stave Five*

## The use of punctuation

Writers use punctuation to guide the reader and create particular effects. For example in the first sentence of Stave Five, Dickens writes: **'Yes! and the bedpost was his own.'** Exclamation marks usually appear at the end of a sentence, but here Dickens does not follow the standard rules. He places the exclamation mark mid-sentence to create an immediate change of tone.

**1** Dickens makes much use of exclamation marks in Stave Five. Find three examples of exclamation marks being used to express feelings.

**2** Examine and comment on the effects of Dickens's use of punctuation in the following extracts:

a **'Do you know whether they've sold the prize turkey hanging up there? – Not the little prize turkey: the big one?'**

b **'Oh, Jacob Marley! Heaven and the Christmastime be praised for this! I say it on my knees, old Jacob; on my knees!'**

c **'Wonderful party, wonderful games, wonderful unanimity, won-der-ful happiness!'**

### ✔ Learning checkpoint

Look again at the scene that takes place in Scrooge's office on the morning after Christmas Day (starting with **'But he was early at the office next morning'** to **'Make up the fires and buy another coalscuttle before you dot another i, Bob Cratchit!'**)

Write a brief essay comparing the way that Dickens presents Scrooge here with the way the **character** is presented in Stave One. Consider:

✔ the ways in which Scrooge at first appears unchanged

✔ evidence of the change that has taken place in him

✔ references to the time

✔ how Dickens makes this scene light-hearted and humorous.

## Why is *A Christmas Carol* so popular?

*A Christmas Carol* was written more than 170 years ago, yet it has never been out of print and is often produced on stage and screen. Look at the following possible explanations for this story's continued popularity.

**A** It reminds us of what is really important in life – not work and making money, but sharing your time and your good fortune with friends and family.

**B** It makes us realise that we all have a bit of Scrooge in us – when we walk past beggars on the street or change the TV channel when charity appeals come on.

**C** It has fantastic descriptions of all the things we traditionally associate with Christmas such as delicious food and Christmas parties.

**D** It reminds us that we are part of a community and if we become disconnected from it, as Scrooge does, we become lesser people.

**E** It is as relevant today, as it was back in 1843. We have food banks and people living on the streets – poverty has not disappeared.

**F** It has lots of dramatic, memorable scenes such as Marley's Ghost with its clanking chains and the Ghost of Christmas Yet to Come pointing Scrooge to his grave.

**G** It makes us think of the parallels with life today – Scrooge's world of 'business' is like the banks of today; Bob Cratchit is on minimum wage and at the mercy of his employer.

**H** It has become part of the tradition of Christmas – everybody likes a good ghost story.

Ⅰ Although Scrooge is miserable and mean, he is also quite a funny, lovable character.

Ｊ It gives hope because it helps us believe that a person can always change no matter how they have behaved or what they have done.

**❶** Work in small groups. Discuss the suggestions for why *A Christmas Carol* remains so popular. Copy and complete the following table to show whether you agree, partly agree or disagree with each explanation. Give your reasons, making sure they are based on evidence from the text.

| Explanation | Agree/partly agree/disagree | Reasons | Evidence |
|---|---|---|---|
| A | partly agree | Scrooge is all work and no play – miserable. Much happier when reconnected to others. Money does matter, as Tony Tim will die without it. | |
| B | | | |
| C | | | |

**❷** Using a grid like this, place the explanations in order, with the one you consider to be most significant at 1 and the one you think least significant at 10.

| 1 | 2 | 3 | 4 | 5 | 6 | 7 | 8 | 9 | 10 |
|---|---|---|---|---|---|---|---|---|---|
| | | | | | | | | | |

**❸** Are there other explanations for the enduring popularity of *A Christmas Carol* that you would like to add? If so, list them.

**❹** Compare your list with a partner and add to it if appropriate.

## GETTING IT INTO WRITING

### Writing about the popularity of *A Christmas Carol*

When you write an answer to a question, it is important that you do not waste time on unnecessary detail.

Read and compare these two openings to the question:

**Why do you think *A Christmas Carol* is still a popular Christmas story in the 21st century?**

### Student A

The story of 'A Christmas Carol' is still very popular and many films have been based on it. One of my favourites is 'Scrooged', which is set in America and in modern times rather than in Victorian times. Another really good version is 'The Muppet Christmas Carol', which closely follows the original although it is funnier than the book. There are also many pantomimes based on Dickens's story, which is about a mean and miserable man called Scrooge who is visited by four ghosts on Christmas Eve. These ghosts change him by showing him his life in the past, the present and the future and by making him realise that his life has not been well-lived. By the end of the story he has changed completely and has become kind, cheerful and charitable ...

### Student B

Dickens wrote 'A Christmas Carol' in 1843 and yet more than 170 years later it is still widely read and adapted for screen and stage productions. There are many reasons that help to explain the enduring popularity of this short Christmas story. The first of these is that, although written almost two centuries ago, the story still has relevance today. Through Scrooge, it portrays a world of business, in which making money is the main concern. As Marley's Ghost regretfully points out, there is ultimately little reward in this: 'The common welfare was my business; charity, mercy, forbearance, and benevolence were, all, my business.' To many, Dickens's world of business resembles the banks today, which appear to put profit before the 'common welfare' ...

**1** Student B offers a better opening to an answer to the question. Explain why.

**2** Now write your own detailed answer in response to the question. Remember to use quotations from the text to back up your points.

✔ **Complete this assignment on Cambridge Elevate.**

## GETTING FURTHER

### 'The Story of the Goblins Who Stole a Sexton'

There are some striking similarities – and differences – between *A Christmas Carol* and 'The Story of the Goblins who Stole a Sexton', which appears in Dickens's first novel, *The Pickwick Papers*, written in 1836–37. The story begins on Christmas Eve when Gabriel Grub is on his way to the churchyard to dig a grave. Like Scrooge, Gabriel Grub is immune to the Christmas cheer around him. However, it is not ghosts but goblins that seek to change Gabriel.

**1** Read the story and identify the ways in which this tale about Gabriel Grub and his experiences is similar to, and different from, Dickens's later story about Scrooge.

✔ **Read 'The Story of the Goblins Who Stole a Sexton' on Cambridge Elevate.**

And so, as Tiny Tim observed, God Bless Us, Every One!

*Stave Five*

# 6

## Plot and structure

How does Dickens take his readers on a journey?

Your progress in this unit:
- understand the plot and timeline
- explore Dickens's use of links and recurring images
- explore the nature and genre of the story.

Dickens wrote *A Christmas Carol* intending for it to be completed and published in time to be sold at Christmas. In his **preface**, he called it a '**Ghostly little book**'. It is much shorter than most of his other stories, and is often referred to as a **novella**.

The **tone** and content of his preface suggest that he hoped the story would entertain his readers by haunting their houses '**pleasantly**'. It also suggests that Dickens wanted to make his readers think by raising '**the Ghost of an Idea**'.

### THE PLOT

### Scrooge's story

The storyline, or plot, is straightforward. The central **character**, Scrooge, is first shown to be a person who treats others badly and has no concern for anything but business and making money. He is visited on Christmas Eve by the ghost of his former business partner, Jacob Marley, who warns him that he needs to change. Marley's Ghost tells Scrooge that he will be haunted by three spirits. These are:

- the Ghost of Christmas Past, which shows Scrooge scenes from his childhood and youth

- the Ghost of Christmas Present, which reveals how Christmas is widely celebrated
- the Ghost of Christmas Yet to Come, which shows Scrooge how his death is not mourned and is, in some places, celebrated

As a result of these visits, Scrooge does indeed change and becomes '**as good a friend, as good a master, and as good a man as the good old City knew**'.

> Watch a summary of the plot on Cambridge Elevate.

### The timeline

The story may be quite simple, but the timeline is more complicated. Scrooge is visited by Marley's Ghost on Christmas Eve. It tells him to expect the first spirit '**tomorrow when the bell tolls one**', to expect the second '**on the next night at the same hour**' and the third '**upon the next night when the last stroke of twelve has ceased to vibrate**'. This would suggest the following timeline:

- **24 December** (Christmas Eve) – Marley's Ghost
- **25 December** (Christmas Day, 1 a.m.) – Ghost of Christmas Past
- **26 December** (Boxing Day, 1 a.m.) – Ghost of Christmas Present
- **26 December** (Boxing Day, midnight) – Ghost of Christmas Yet to Come.

If time had followed its expected sequence, Stave Five would have opened on the morning of the 27 December, but it starts on Christmas Day. The three nights have been compressed into one single night. This change to the normal flow of time helps to emphasise the supernatural powers of the spirits. Like Scrooge, the reader can only conclude: **'The Spirits have done it all in one night. They can do anything they like. Of course they can**.'

> **Watch actors discuss the timeline of *A Christmas Carol* on Cambridge Elevate.**

## STRUCTURE

*A Christmas Carol* is organised into five staves, or chapters. The events take place over one night, from Christmas Eve to Christmas morning. Dickens creates strong links between the five staves, and they are used in part to help the reader trace the gradual change in Scrooge.

The most evident links focus on Bob Cratchit and Scrooge's nephew, Fred:

| | Bob Cratchit | Scrooge's nephew |
|---|---|---|
| **Stave One:** Marley's Ghost | introduced as Scrooge's badly treated clerk | invites Scrooge to Christmas dinner; Scrooge refuses |
| **Stave Two:** The First of the Three Spirits | after old Fezziwig's ball, Scrooge wishes he could have a word or two with his clerk | referred to as the only child of Scrooge's beloved sister Fan; Scrooge seems uneasy |
| **Stave Three:** The Second of the Three Spirits | shown with his family celebrating Christmas; Scrooge is concerned for Tiny Tim | shown with his family celebrating Christmas; Scrooge joins in the games enthusiastically |
| **Stave Four:** The Last of the Spirits | shown with his family mourning the death of Tiny Tim | treats Bob Cratchit with 'extraordinary kindness' after the death of Tiny Tim |
| **Stave Five:** The End of It | Scrooge promises to raise his salary and help his struggling family | Scrooge nervously visits his home, is welcomed and has a wonderful time |

> **Key terms**

> **novella:** a literary term for a work that is too long to be a short story, but shorter than a conventional novel.

## Recurring imagery

In addition to making links through characters and events, Dickens also uses recurring **imagery**. In Stave One, for example, the first indication for Scrooge of what is to come is Marley's face appearing on his door knocker. The reader is reminded of this in Stave Five, when the knocker again catches Scrooge's eye and he declares, **'I shall love it as long as I live'**.

Curtains are another recurring image:

- **Stave Two:** the curtains of Scrooge's bed are drawn around him and then **'drawn aside'** by the hand of the ghost.
- **Stave Three:** Scrooge puts the curtains aside **'with his own hands'**.
- **Stave Four:** the curtains are stolen and sold **'rings and all'**.
- **Stave Five:** Scrooge discovers that the curtains **'are not torn down'**. He takes this as a sign: **'They are here – I am here – the shadows of the things that would have been may be dispelled.'** Here, the curtains signify to both Scrooge and the reader that he is now firmly back in the 'real' world.

## Genre

There are many different **genres** of story. In 1843, ghost stories were becoming increasingly popular and A Christmas Carol has some of the traditional elements associated with a ghost story: the central character is haunted by ghosts; bells ring mysteriously; the ghosts possess super-human powers. It also draws on some of the gothic traditions of late 18th-century ghost stories – a literary style characterised by gloom, the grotesque and the supernatural. This is perhaps most evident in Dickens's portrayal of Marley's Ghost, with its clanking chains, transparent body and **'lower jaw dropped down upon its breast'**. It is also evident in the description of the phantoms that fill the air at the end of Stave One and in the portrayal of the Ghost of Christmas Yet to Come.

However, A Christmas Carol is a ghost story with a difference. Marley is the only ghost of a person who once lived. The other three are spirits of Christmas. While Marley and the Ghost of Christmas Yet to Come show some traditional frightening features of ghosts, the Ghosts of Christmas Past and Christmas Present are more endearing characters. They are not devised to frighten Scrooge but to guide and instruct him. Furthermore, many of the scenes in A Christmas Carol are joyful, such as old Fezziwig's ball and Christmas Eve at Fred's home. There is plenty here to remind the reader that Christmas is a time of celebration, and to ensure that this story haunts readers' houses pleasantly.

### Key terms

**imagery:** language intended to conjure up a vivid picture in the reader's mind.

**genre:** the kind or type of literature to which a text belongs; stories within a particular genre will have similar characteristics.

Finding that he turned uncomfortably cold when he began to wonder which of his curtains this new spectre would draw back, he put every one aside with his own hands …

*Stave Three*

## Allegory

In some ways *A Christmas Carol* is similar to a fairytale. Early in Stave One, Dickens uses the traditional fairytale opening, 'Once upon a time', and at the end of the story the reader is left with the sense that everyone lived happily ever after.

However, the story has stronger foundations in the traditions of **allegory**. Scrooge at first represents values that are opposed to the idea of Christmas – greed, selfishness and a lack of goodwill – while the Cratchits represent the poor, deserving of sympathy and a better quality of life. The Ghost of Christmas Past can be seen as representing memory. It '**fluctuated in its distinctness**', much as most memories do. The Ghost of Christmas Present symbolises the abundance, generosity and good cheer traditionally associated with Christmas. With the Ghost of Christmas Yet to Come comes the suggestion of death and the moral reckoning that accompanies it.

> **Find out more about allegory on Cambridge Elevate.**

## DEVELOP AND REVISE

### Identify links in the story

**1** Answer the following questions:

  **a** Two portly gentlemen ask Scrooge for money in Stave One. Under what circumstances does one of these gentlemen appear in Stave Five?

  **b** In conversation with the two portly gentlemen, Scrooge speaks of the poor being sent to prisons or workhouses or of dying and '**decreasing the surplus population**'. When and why are these words thrown back at him?

  **c** The carol singer is threatened with a ruler by Scrooge in Stave One. What reference is made to him in Stave Two?

  **d** Jacob Marley and his ghost play a significant part in Stave One. What reference is made to him in Stave Five?

**2** The links you have identified draw the reader's attention to changes that have taken or are taking place in Scrooge. For each one, write a developed comment on its significance.

## Explore imagery

**1** In Stave One, Marley's Ghost tells Scrooge:

> 'Expect the first tomorrow when the bell tolls one. Expect the second on the next night at the same hour. The third upon the next night when the last stroke of twelve has ceased to vibrate.'

Marley's Ghost: Stave One

Write a paragraph explaining how Dickens uses the chiming of bells to introduce each of the three spirits. Remember – the third spirit appears at the end of Stave Three.

**2** In Stave One, every bell in Scrooge's house rings, making him feel a '**strange, inexplicable dread**'. How does Scrooge feel about the ringing of the church bells in Stave Five?

**3** Images of food are used throughout the story. How are they used to suggest:

  **a** the generosity of old Fezziwig
  **b** ideas of abundance and plenty associated with the Ghost of Christmas Present
  **c** the poverty of the Cratchits?

## Is this a ghost story?

**1** Use what you have learnt in this unit and your own ideas to write a short essay in answer to this question:

**To what extent do you think *A Christmas Carol* is a ghost story?**

> **Key terms**
>
> **allegory:** a story, poem or painting in which the apparent meaning of the characters and events is used to symbolise a deeper moral or spiritual meaning.

# Context and setting

## How does Dickens bring the setting and action alive?

## CHARLES DICKENS

Dickens was already a well-known and popular writer by the time he published *A Christmas Carol* in December 1843. Up to this point, his novels, such as *The Pickwick Papers* and *Oliver Twist*, had been published in monthly instalments. *A Christmas Carol*, however, was published as a complete **novella**.

Dickens was a great believer in social reform, and *A Christmas Carol* reflects many of his concerns regarding the plight of the poor. It also draws on his own life experiences. He had a sister called Fanny who died young, as did Scrooge's sister Fan. Dickens also had a brother called Frederick – the name of Scrooge's nephew. As a child, he had experienced loneliness and developed a love of reading, as we see Scrooge do on his journey with the Ghost of Christmas Past. *The Arabian Nights* and *Robinson Crusoe*, referred to in Stave Two, were two of his favourite books. When Dickens was 12, his father was imprisoned for debt – the same threat faced by the family in Stave Four.

## SETTING

*A Christmas Carol* is set against the background of the City of London and makes specific references to places such as St Paul's Churchyard, Cornhill and Camden town. However, for the most part, the place has little direct impact on the story. The street scenes described in Stave One and Stave Three could be those of any city streets on Christmas morning.

### The weather

One significant feature of the setting is the weather, and cold and fog are referred to several times in the text:

**Stave One:** 'It was cold, bleak, biting weather' and 'The fog came pouring in at every chink and keyhole'.

**Stave Two:** When Scrooge looks through his window, 'it was still very foggy and extremely cold'. However, when the ghost takes him to scenes from his past, 'the mist had vanished with it, for it was a clear, cold, winter day'.

**Stave Three:** 'The sky was gloomy, and the shortest streets were choked up with a dingy mist'.

**Stave Five:** when Scrooge opens his window, there is 'No fog, no mist; clear bright, jovial, stirring cold'.

The weather may have symbolic significance. How might these references to the weather reflect Scrooge's personality and how it changes?

# CONTEXT

## Poverty

A Christmas Carol should be seen in the **context** of life in Britain in the 19th century. As a result of the Industrial Revolution, people moved to the towns and cities in search of employment. Wages were low and working conditions were poor. There was much overcrowding and slums were often situated close to areas of great wealth, as described in Stave Four. The Poor Law Amendment Act of 1834 meant that the only help available to many of the poor was the workhouse.

Many Victorians believed that there were 'deserving' and 'undeserving' poor. The deserving poor were those who experienced poverty through no fault of their own; the undeserving poor were those who were thought to be poor because of laziness or personal problems. In Stave One, Scrooge thinks that all poor people are undeserving, and refuses to give money to help them.

Dickens was angered by the plight of the poor and by how they were treated by the wealthy in socity. In Stave Three, the child Want signifies the extreme poverty of some children. In the portrayal of the thieves in Stave Four, Dickens suggests that the attitudes of the rich breed contempt and crime amongst the poor: '**Every person has a right to take care of themselves.** *He* **always did!**'

## Education

At the start of the 19th century, very few children went to school. Most poor children worked. Although factory owners were supposed to provide at least two hours' education every day for child-workers, this rarely happened. In general, only the wealthy could afford to give their children a good education.

Dickens was in favour of education for all. He was a strong supporter of 'Ragged Schools' – schools for the poorest children – and believed that education 'is the one thing needful' to resolve evil. These views are reflected in Stave Four, where the Ghost of Christmas Present blames Man for the children, Ignorance and Want, and warns that on the brow of Ignorance he sees the word 'Doom'.

## Business

By 1843, London had become the world's largest city and a global political, financial and trading capital. The world of business thrived. It might be argued that Scrooge represents this rather cold world, driven by money, and that Dickens opposed it. However, this view does not present the full picture. Old Fezziwig was a man of business, but is shown as a generous and kind employer, loved by his workforce. Perhaps Dickens is suggesting that those who have money and power have a responsibility to help those less well-off. What do you think?

It seems that the problem with Scrooge and his one-time partner, Jacob Marley, is not that they made money from business, but that making money became their sole aim in life. Scrooge is mean and unkind to his clerk but he also has no joy in his own life. He has cut himself off from the world and believes that paying his taxes relieves him of any further duty to the poor.

### Key terms

**context:** the historical circumstances of a piece of writing, which affect what an author wrote and the way they wrote it.

## Christmas traditions

Today, *A Christmas Carol* seems to embody all the traditions associated with Christmas – from the family gatherings and charitable donations to the holly wreath on the head of the Ghost of Christmas Present and the Christmas pudding eaten by the Cratchits. However, for the Victorian reader, many of these traditions were in decline. One consequence of the Industrial Revolution was that many people moved to the large cities, leaving their cultural traditions behind. In the cities, many employers were unwilling to give employees a day of paid holiday and factories were often kept open on Christmas Day.

When *A Christmas Carol* was published, it revived much of the nostalgia and tradition associated with Christmas. The story's popularity resulted in many of the customs and traditions it describes becoming part of the Christmas season once more.

## DEVELOP AND REVISE

Watch a discussion about how the story has influenced Christmas on Cambridge Elevate.

### Attitudes towards the poor

1 The notion of the 'deserving' and 'undeserving' poor is a frequent topic of political debate today. Work in small groups to discuss the following questions to help you explore the relevance of this subject.

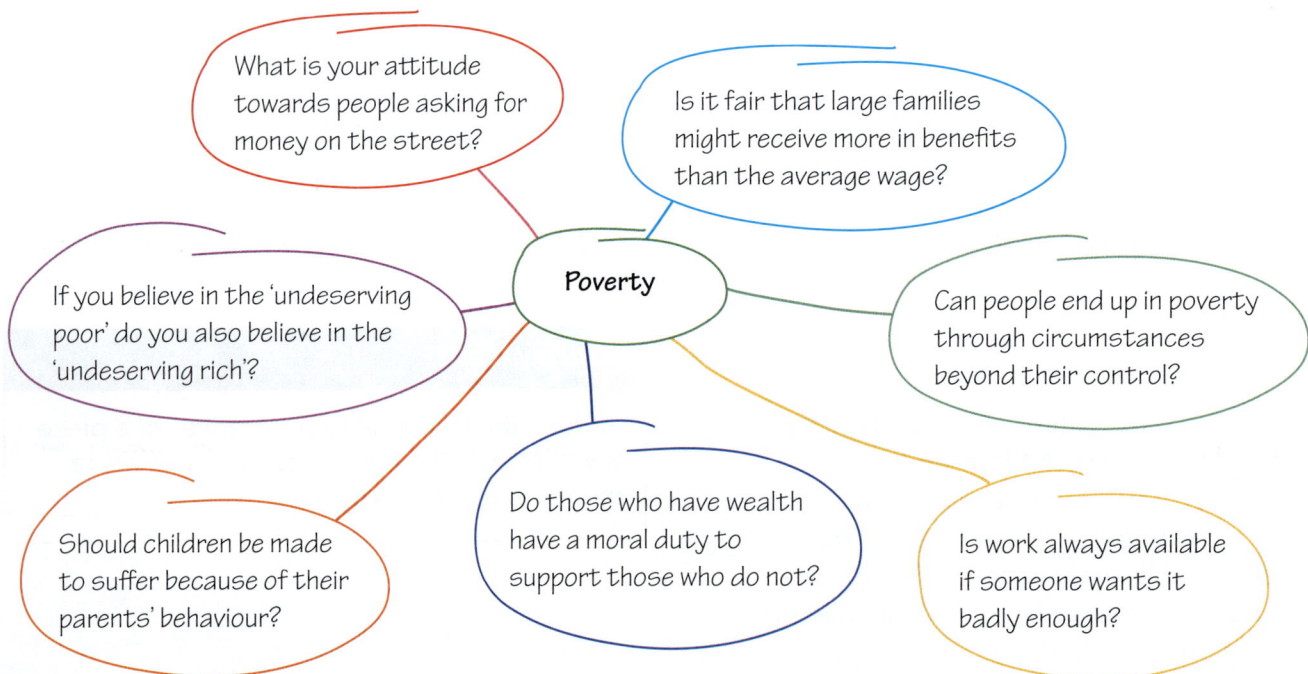

What is your attitude towards people asking for money on the street?

Is it fair that large families might receive more in benefits than the average wage?

If you believe in the 'undeserving poor' do you also believe in the 'undeserving rich'?

**Poverty**

Can people end up in poverty through circumstances beyond their control?

Should children be made to suffer because of their parents' behaviour?

Do those who have wealth have a moral duty to support those who do not?

Is work always available if someone wants it badly enough?

2 Think again about *A Christmas Carol*. What does it suggest about Dickens's attitude to the poor and to the responsibilities of the wealthy towards them? Support your ideas with reference to the text.

## Understanding context

**1** Read the following quotations. For each one identify:

**a** who says it
**b** the context in which it appears
**c** what it reveals about Scrooge and his attitude to money and/or business.

### Stave One

'It's enough for a man to understand his own business, and not to interfere with other people's'

'And yet, you don't think me ill-used when I pay a day's wages for no work.'

### Stave Two

'He has the power to render us happy or unhappy; to make our service light or burdensome; a pleasure or a toil […] The happiness he gives is quite as great as if it cost a fortune.'

'I have seen your nobler aspirations fall off one by one, until the master passion, Gain, engrosses you.'

### Stave Three

'His wealth is of no use to him. He don't do any good with it.'

### Stave Four

'But, before that time, we shall be ready with the money; and, even though we were not, it would be bad fortune indeed to find so merciless a creditor in his successor.'

### Stave Five

'If you please, not a farthing less. A great many back payments are included in it, I assure you.'

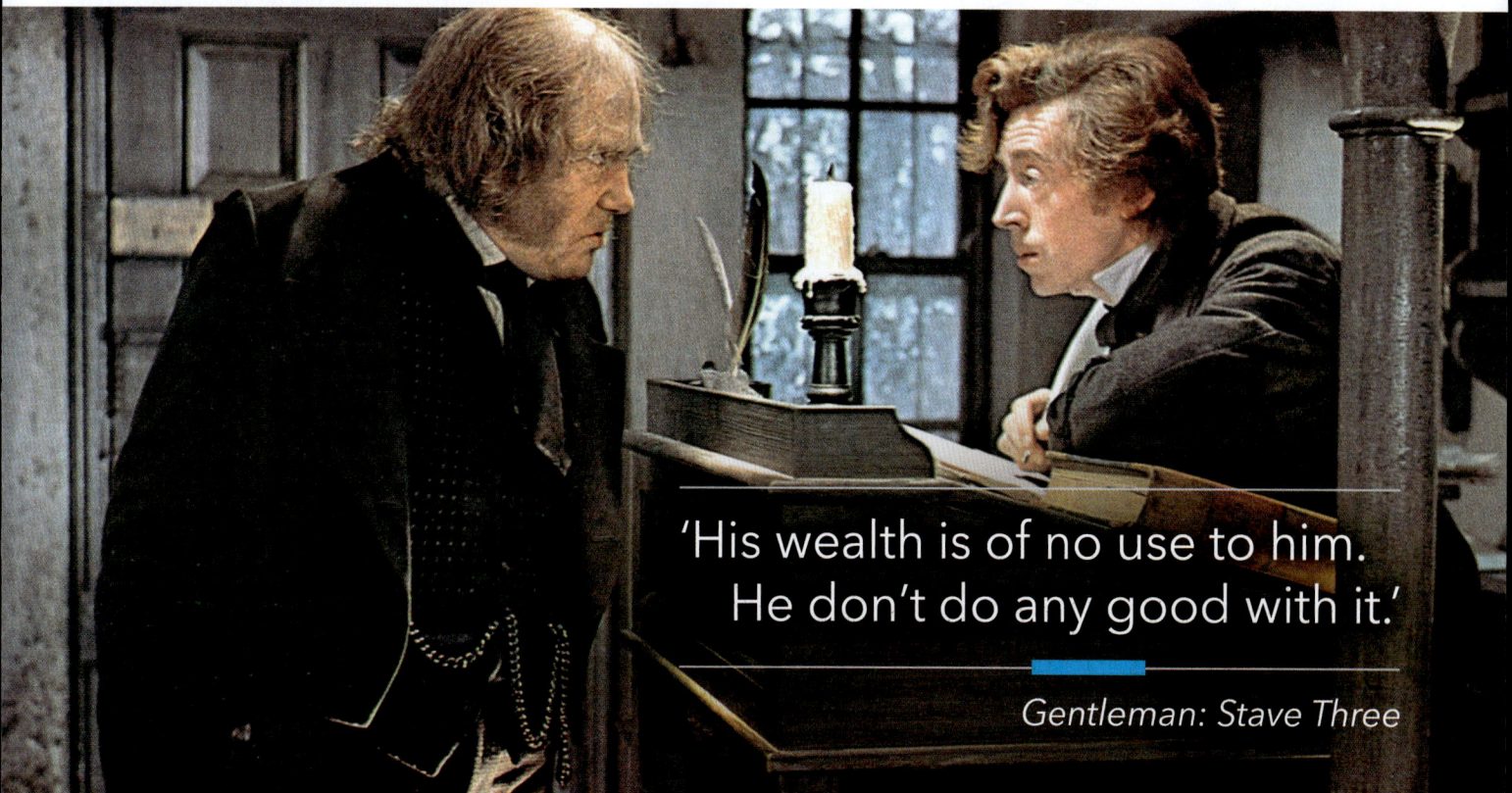

'His wealth is of no use to him. He don't do any good with it.'

*Gentleman: Stave Three*

# 8

# Character and characterisation

## How does Dickens create memorable characters?

Your progress in this unit:

- examine how other characters revolve around Scrooge
- explore how Dickens shows the 'reclamation' of Scrooge
- explore the distinct characteristics and roles of the four Ghosts
- consider the significance of minor characters.

In *A Christmas Carol*, Dickens created a number of memorable **characters**. The most distinctive of these is, of course, Scrooge, and we often only see glimpses of other characters in relation to him.

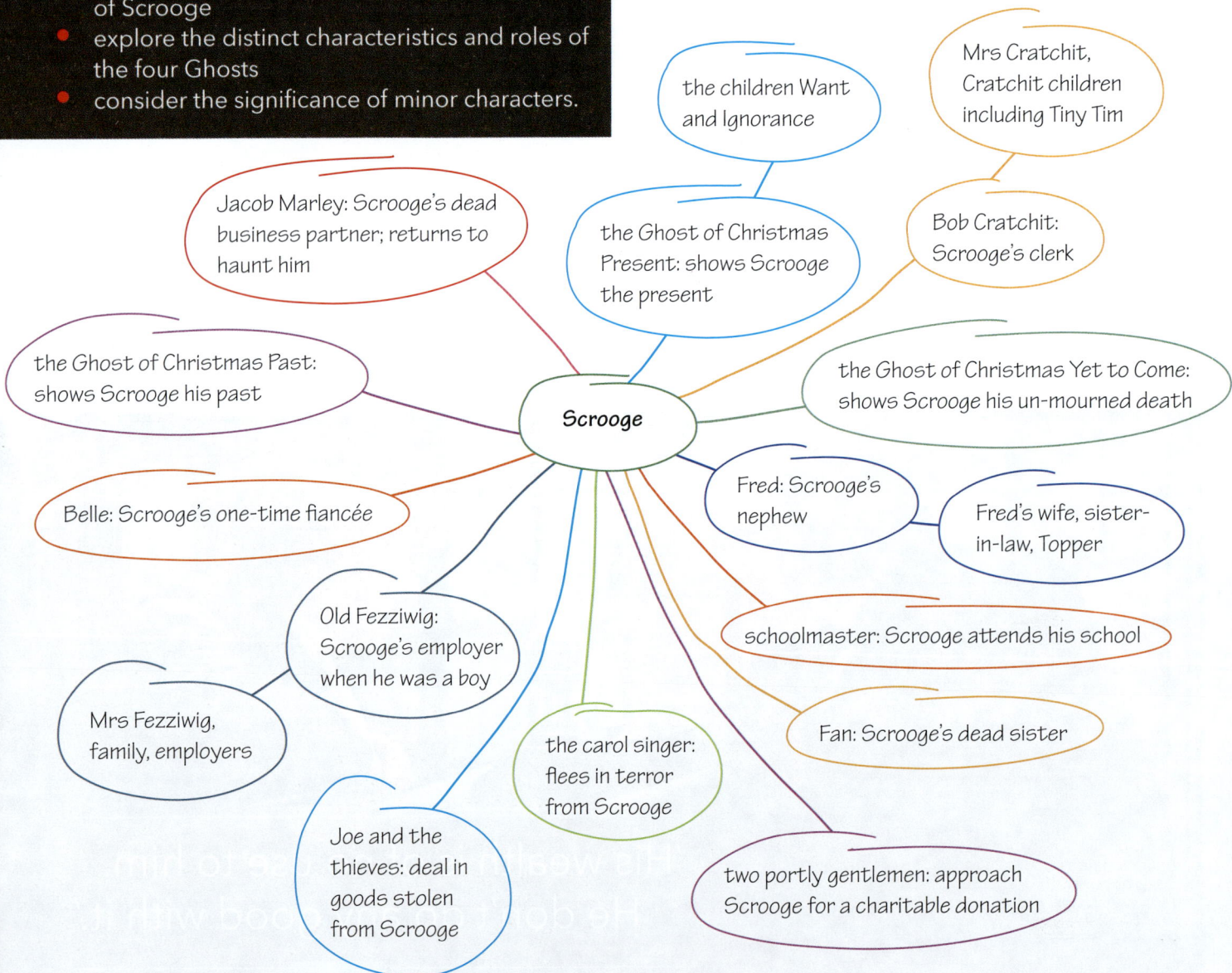

the children Want and Ignorance

Mrs Cratchit, Cratchit children including Tiny Tim

Jacob Marley: Scrooge's dead business partner; returns to haunt him

the Ghost of Christmas Present: shows Scrooge the present

Bob Cratchit: Scrooge's clerk

the Ghost of Christmas Past: shows Scrooge his past

**Scrooge**

the Ghost of Christmas Yet to Come: shows Scrooge his un-mourned death

Belle: Scrooge's one-time fiancée

Fred: Scrooge's nephew

Fred's wife, sister-in-law, Topper

Old Fezziwig: Scrooge's employer when he was a boy

schoolmaster: Scrooge attends his school

Mrs Fezziwig, family, employers

the carol singer: flees in terror from Scrooge

Fan: Scrooge's dead sister

Joe and the thieves: deal in goods stolen from Scrooge

two portly gentlemen: approach Scrooge for a charitable donation

## SCROOGE

### Scrooge in Stave One

At the start, Dickens **characterises** Scrooge as a man with few redeeming features. He does this by:

- direct description: '**a squeezing, wrenching, grasping, scraping, clutching, covetous, old sinner!**'
- comparing him with elements of weather: '**No wind that blew was bitterer than he, no falling snow was more intent upon its purpose.**'
- showing how he relates to others: his nephew, his clerk, the portly gentlemen and a carol singer
- showing how others relate to him: '**No beggars asked him to bestow a trifle, no children asked him what it was o'clock.**'
- recording Scrooge's words: '**If they would rather die, they had better do it, and decrease the surplus population.**'

However, there are hints at another, more appealing, side to Scrooge. His almost twisted sense of humour makes the reader suspect that he has somewhere, locked inside him, a capacity for fun. This is evident when he says that '**every idiot who goes about with "Merry Christmas" on his lips should be boiled with his own pudding, and buried with a stake of holly through his heart**' and his joke that there is '**more of gravy than of the grave**' about Marley's Ghost. Dickens also hints at Scrooge's vulnerability by showing him in his dressing gown, slippers and nightcap sitting in front of a low fire after checking that nobody is hiding in his apartments.

### Scrooge's 'reclamation'

The Ghost of Christmas Past tells Scrooge that its business is his '**reclamation**'. The word suggests that rather than being changed, his real self will be allowed to emerge. From this point on, Scrooge never again behaves or speaks in the same mean manner that he does in Stave One. As the story progresses, Dickens gradually reveals this true self. He builds a picture of Scrooge's past for the reader and shows how Scrooge responds to these 'forgotten' memories. Scrooge's response is shown through narrative, describing how he behaves, and direct speech, putting his responses in his own words.

Narrative:

During the whole of this time Scrooge had acted like a man out of his wits.

Direct speech:

'Why, it's old Fezziwig! Bless his heart, it's Fezziwig alive again!'

How does Dickens suggest that Scrooge was changing in these two quotations?

### DEVELOP AND REVISE

1 What other examples can you find in *A Christmas Carol* that show Scrooge's 'reclamation'? Look for examples of both narrative and direct speech, and make a list in a table like this.

| Examples of narrative | Examples of direct speech |
| --- | --- |
| | |
| | |
| | |

2 A student has suggested that 'In Stave Five the reader sees the real Mr Scrooge. We finally get to like him.' How far would you agree or disagree with this student? Use quotations from the table and the rest of the book to support your answer.

### Key terms

**characterise:** to describe features that are unique or distinctive.

## OTHER CHARACTERS

### Scrooge's nephew, Fred

Through Fred, Dickens presents the reader with a direct contrast to Scrooge. Points of contrast include:

- images of heat: 'He had so heated himself with rapid walking in the fog and frost […] that he was all in a glow'.
- he married for love and is happy in his marriage
- he 'revelled' in laughter
- he understands that Christmas is 'a kind, forgiving, charitable, pleasant time'.
- he is kind to others, as shown in his words to Bob after Tiny Tim's death.

Although Scrooge treats him harshly, Fred stands up to Scrooge. It could be that, in creating this character, Dickens wanted to show the reader the kind of person Scrooge could have been.

### Bob Cratchit

Through Bob Cratchit, Scrooge's roughly treated clerk, Dickens shows the reader that there can be happiness in poverty if there is also love. Bob Cratchit has much that Scrooge lacks – a capacity for fun, a loving family, contentment. Despite his grief at the death of Tiny Tim, he is 'reconciled to what had happened'. His loyalty to his employer, shown in his Christmas toast, is finally repaid when Scrooge promises to raise his salary and help his family.

> Watch a character interview with Bob Cratchit on Cambridge Elevate.

### The minor characters

Dickens fills the pages of *A Christmas Carol* with a host of minor characters. Dickens creates a distinctive identity for each one and, collectively, they add life, colour and sometimes humour to the text. There are many minor characters in the story. One of the most memorable of these is Tiny Tim. He has only a small part in the text, but it is significant in terms of Scrooge's reclamation. He represents the 'surplus population' that Scrooge derides but has never encountered face to face. An invalid child, Tiny Tim is very close to his father, treasured by his family and seems wise beyond his years. He has a profound effect on Scrooge, and the narrator declares that his 'childish essence was from God'. It is his words that mark the end of the story.

> Watch a video about how Dickens establishes minor characters on Cambridge Elevate.

## DEVELOP AND REVISE

### The four ghosts

1. The four ghosts have individual characteristics and distinct roles to play in Scrooge's reclamation. Look at the following descriptions. Find evidence in the story to support each statement in each sketch.

#### Marley's Ghost

Marley is the only ghost to have lived a human life. He had been Scrooge's partner and had died seven years earlier. The Ghost wears the chain Marley made in life. It is a frightening and eerie figure. Marley only discovered his mistakes in life after he had died. The ghost offers Scrooge the chance to avoid its fate. Scrooge's response to Marley's Ghost changes over the course of its visit.

#### The Ghost of Christmas Past

The appearance of this ghost is not fixed but ever-changing. It makes its purpose clear to Scrooge before transporting him to his past. It gently draws out Scrooge's emotional responses to his boyhood memories. The ghost's challenge about old Fezziwig's actions makes Scrooge defend his generosity. It can be forceful. Finally, it shows Scrooge not who he was, but who he could have been.

### The Ghost of Christmas Present

The description of this ghost emphasises its freedom. It is associated with abundance. It offers Scrooge a view into the homes of people he knows. It shows Scrooge how he is regarded by those who know him. The ghost also connects Scrooge with others in society not personally known to him. It uses Scrooge's words from Stave One against him. It reveals the consequences of Man's failure to provide for the poor. This ghost is capable of anger. Its form changes in the course of the night.

### The Ghost of Christmas Yet to Come

This ghost is frightening and mysterious. It communicates with Scrooge, but not with words. It shows Scrooge the impact his death has on others. It also shows Scrooge a mourned death. The ghost seems unmoved by Scrooge's distress until the end. The ghost's form changes at the end Stave Four.

## Examine the minor characters

**1** Choose five of the following minor characters. For each one, write a brief outline explaining:

**a** what you are shown about them
**b** the methods Dickens uses to present them.

| | |
|---|---|
| the carol singer | the thieves |
| Fan | Mrs Cratchit |
| Mrs Fezziwig | Joe |
| Belle | the two portly gentlemen |
| the schoolmaster | Want and Ignorance |
| Peter Cratchit | the businessmen |
| Martha Cratchit | |
| Topper | |

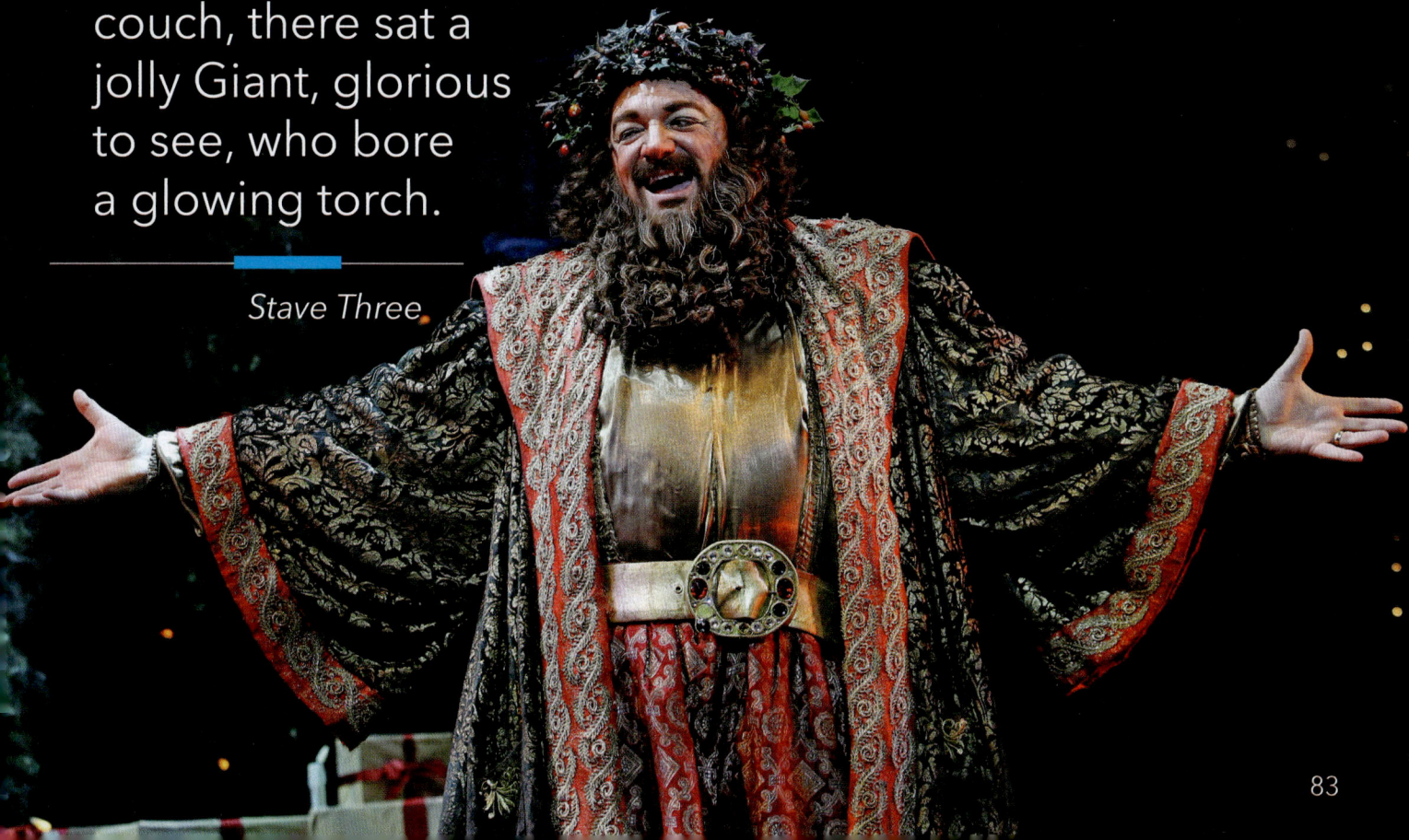

In easy state upon this couch, there sat a jolly Giant, glorious to see, who bore a glowing torch.

*Stave Three*

# 9

## Themes and ideas

### What big ideas dominate the story?

Your progress in this unit:

- consider the impact of the narrator's perspective
- explore ideas connected with religion
- investigate Dickens's views on childhood
- examine ideas linked with wealth, poverty and happiness.

## THE NARRATOR'S PERSPECTIVE

While Dickens's views on social issues seem evident throughout the story of *A Christmas Carol*, the story itself is told through the **narrator** who has his own distinct personality and opinions. For example when describing the fiddler at old Fezziwig's ball, the narrator says he was '**the sort of man who knew his business better than you or I could have told it him!**' When describing Fred's laugh he comments: '**If you should happen, by any unlikely chance, to know a man more blessed in a laugh than Scrooge's nephew, all I can say is, I should like to know him too.**' Observations such as these add a personal touch to the narrative. They build the sense of a person telling the story to a listening audience, much as stories were told around the fireside in Victorian times.

Occasionally, the narrator's asides may sound uncomfortable to a 21st-century reader. For example his comments on Fred's wife may sound patronising and sexist to a modern reader. However, they should be read in the **context** in which they were written – a time when women had a limited public life and were not allowed to vote.

## KEY THEMES

### Religion

*A Christmas Carol* is set at Christmas, the Christian festival that marks the birth of Christ. It was written at a time when most people in Britain were Christian. Even so, there are very few direct references to Christ's birth. Marley's Ghost refers to '**that blessed Star which led the Wise Men to a poor abode**'. Fred refers to the '**veneration due**' to the '**sacred name and origin**' of Christmas, and the narrator reminds us that it is '**good to be children sometimes, and never better than at Christmas, when its mighty Founder was a child himself**'. In Stave Three, on Christmas Day the '**steeples called good people all to church and chapel**' and Bob Cratchit and Tiny Tim return from Church.

Despite its limited references to the birth of Christ, *A Christmas Carol* is firmly embedded in Christian values. According to the Bible, Christ helped the poor and also stressed the importance of children. The Ghost of Christmas Present takes Scrooge to '**almshouse, hospital and gaol**' in order to teach Scrooge the true meaning of Christmas. This spirit also shelters the children Want and Ignorance under its cloak and, when Scrooge realises that Tiny Tim is dead, he recalls words from the Bible that focus on children.

Dickens was Christian, but he criticised those who thought that teaching the poor religious values was more important than feeding and educating them. He shows this when the Ghost of Christmas Present, angered by Scrooge's accusation that it seeks to close shops on Sundays, says:

'There are some upon this earth of yours who lay claim to know us, and who do their deeds of passion, pride, ill will, hatred, envy, bigotry, and selfishness in our name, who are as strange to us, and all our kith and kin, as if they had never lived.'

Ghost of Christmas Present: Stave Three

**Watch a discussion about the influence of Christianity on Cambridge Elevate.**

## Redemption

Redemption – the belief that no matter how bad a person is in their life, they can still be forgiven and go to Heaven if they truly repent – is an important feature of Christianity. For Marley, it is too late for redemption: '**if that spirit goes not forth in life, it is condemned to do so after death**'. However, Marley's Ghost offers Scrooge a chance to avoid this same fate.

The Ghost of Christmas Past reminds Scrooge what it is like to feel both joy and sadness. The Ghost of Christmas Present connects him with the feelings and experiences of others. However, it is the Ghost of Christmas Yet to Come that finally brings about true repentance and allows Scrooge the chance to '**sponge away the writing on this stone**'.

## Wealth, poverty and happiness

While the Industrial Revolution brought huge prosperity to Britain, it also brought great inequality with many people living in poverty. There is no evidence in the story to suggest that Dickens opposed the possession of wealth; however, it is clear that he believed wealth brought responsibilities. Marley's failure to use his wealth responsibly results in an eternity of

'**incessant torture of remorse**'. At the start of the story, Scrooge is heading in the same direction. He demonstrates a callous attitude towards the poor. He believes that he does enough simply by paying his taxes and has no time for charity. In contrast, the two portly gentlemen show an active concern for the poor, and old Fezziwig is shown to be a kind and generous employer.

Dickens presents a range of views about money:

**Money does not equal happiness**
Scrooge has money but lost the chance of a happy marriage, resulting in the joyless life he leads in Stave One.

**Money can bring happiness**
Old Fezziwig uses his money to throw a ball for the enjoyment of others.

**Poverty does not equal unhappiness**
Bob Cratchit earns little, but he and his family are happy.

**Money can change lives**
Without money to pay a doctor, Tiny Tim will die.
Without some money, people are condemned to the prisons and workhouses.
Without some money, childhood is stifled (Want and Ignorance).

**Watch a video which shows that poverty does not equal unhappiness on Cambridge Elevate.**

## DEVELOP AND REVISE

### See things from the narrator's point of view

**1** Investigate the narrator's perspective by reading what he says:

a about the phrase **'as dead as a doornail'** at the start of Stave One

b when watching Belle's daughter play with the younger children

c when the Ghost of Christmas Present blesses Bob's house.

Write a paragraph explaining how his observations add a personal voice to the story.

### Explore the role of children

**1** Childhood and children have an important role in *A Christmas Carol*. How are the following qualities demonstrated by the named children?

a vulnerability: Scrooge as a child

b innocence: Little Fan

c joy: Belle's children

d wisdom: Tiny Tim.

**2** Explain how Want and Ignorance represent the neglect and ill-treatment of children. Think about:

a How they are described

b What the ghost says about them.

Spirit of Tiny Tim, thy childish essence was from God!

*Stave Four*

## Investigate the theme of money

**1** The quotations in the table relate to money. Identify the context
in which each one is said and comment on its significance.

| Quotation | Context | Significance |
|---|---|---|
| 'What reason have you to be morose? You're rich enough.' (Stave One) | Fred responds to Scrooge's accusation that he has no reason to be merry because he is poor. | Fred's response challenges Scrooge's automatic association of money with happiness. Although Fred is Scrooge's first visitor, the truth of what he says is already clear to the reader; wealth has not made Scrooge happy. It also highlights the **contrast** between Scrooge and his nephew. |
| 'Many thousands are in want of common necessaries; hundreds of thousands are in want of common comforts.' (Stave One) | | |
| 'The dealings of my trade were but a drop of water in the comprehensive ocean of my business!' (Stave One) | | |
| 'The happiness he gives is quite as great as if it cost a fortune.' (Stave Two) | | |
| 'Our contract is an old one. It was made when we were both poor, and content to be so, until, in good season, we could improve our worldly fortune.' (Stave Two) | | |
| 'The Founder of the Feast, indeed! I wish I had him here. I'd give him a piece of my mind to feast upon.' (Stave Three) | | |
| 'His wealth is no use to him. He don't do any good with it.' (Stave Three) | | |
| 'He frightened every one away when he was alive, to profit us when he was dead!' Stave Four | | |
| 'It would be bad fortune indeed to find so merciless a creditor in his successor.' (Stave Four) | | |
| 'Not a farthing less. A great many back payments are included in it, I assure you.' (Stave Five) | | |

# 10

## Language

### Why does the language have such impact?

### VOICE AND DETAIL

In *A Christmas Carol*, Dickens creates a world of mystery, ghostliness and Christmas celebration. It is a world that moves rapidly from one time and place to another – and one inhabited by **characters** as diverse as Tiny Tim and old Joe. It is also a world that has been reinvented many times on stage and screen. Dickens creates such a dramatic and popular world through his skill with language and the manipulation of words to achieve specific effects.

### The voice of the narrator

At times, the **narrator** is a formal observer and recorder of events. At these times, Dickens writes in the third person and in a fairly formal **tone**:

Scrooge reverently disclaimed all intention to offend or any knowledge of having willfully 'bonneted' the Spirit at any period of his life. He then made bold to inquire what business brought him there.

Stave Two

At other times, Dickens gives the narrator a more informal voice. He addresses the reader directly, using a conversational tone and giving his personal views. In these cases, the writing is in the first person:

At last, however, he began to think – as you or I would have thought at first; for it is always the person not in the predicament who knows what ought to have been done in it, and would unquestionably have done it too – at last, I say, he began to …

Stave Three

### Dickens's use of detail

Dickens packs his sentences with detail, choosing his words carefully to build a picture for the reader:

It was cold, bleak, biting weather: foggy withal: and he could hear the people in the court outside go wheezing up and down, beating their hands upon their breasts, and stamping their feet upon the pavement stones to warm them.

Stave One

Adjectives convey the weather.
Verbs convey the people's actions.

He tells the reader a great deal about a minor character in just a few lines, as in this description of a member of the Lord Mayor's household in Stave One:

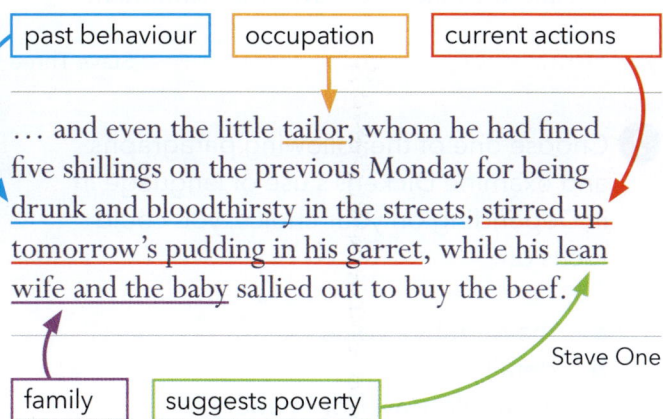

| past behaviour | occupation | current actions |

… and even the little <u>tailor</u>, whom he had fined five shillings on the previous Monday for being <u>drunk and bloodthirsty in the streets</u>, <u>stirred up tomorrow's pudding in his garret</u>, while his <u>lean wife and the baby</u> sallied out to buy the beef.

Stave One

| family | suggests poverty |

Paragraphs are similarly packed with detail. Read again the paragraph in which Belle's husband arrives home and is greeted by his children. Note how carefully Dickens describes the scene to create a sense of chaos and of joy.

## LANGUAGE FEATURES

### Lists

Dickens makes extensive use of lists. Sometimes these occur within sentences, piling up details to build a picture in the reader's mind. At other times, they occur in paragraphs. Look at the paragraph in which Dickens describes the Ghost of Christmas Past in Stave Two, for example. How does he use a list to build a picture of the ghost? What effect does the final sentence of the paragraph have?

### Repetition

At times, Dickens repeats a single word or phrase to create a particular effect. For example when describing Scrooge in Stave One he writes: '**No warmth could warm, no wintry weather chill him.**' This is quickly followed by: '**No beggars implored him to bestow a trifle, no children asked him what it was o'clock …**' Think about what the repetition of the word 'no' tells us about Scrooge's character.

Similarly, when describing the people arriving at old Fezziwig's ball, Dickens starts eight consecutive sentences with the words '**In came**' to separate the distinctive groups of participants and the ninth with '**In they all came**' to show them collectively.

Watch a dramatic reading of old Fezziwig's ball on Cambridge Elevate.

Find out more about Dickens's use of linguistic features on Cambridge Elevate.

### Imagery

Dickens frequently uses **imagery** in his descriptions. His choices help the reader picture something more precisely or understand an idea more fully. For example what are the effects of the use of **personification** and **simile** in the sentence: '**The owner of one scant nose, gnawed and mumbled by the hungry cold as bones are gnawed by dogs**'? What is the effect of the **metaphor** in the phrase '**although the court was of the narrowest, the houses opposite were mere phantoms**'?

### Sounds

Dickens frequently refers to the sounds of church bells and clock chimes to mark both the passage of time and the change in Scrooge. In Stave One, after Scrooge turns the two portly gentlemen away, there is reference to a '**gruff old bell**' which bears characteristics of Scrooge. It is '**gruff**', a word associated with a harsh and surly manner, and the simile is used to emphasise the cold weather.

In contrast, in Stave Five, Scrooge is '**checked in his transports by the churches ringing out the lustiest peals he had ever heard. Clash, clang, hammer; ding, dong, bell! Bell, dong, ding; hammer, clang, clash! Oh, glorious, glorious!**' Dickens's choice of the **adjective** 'lustiest' and use of the **onomatopoeic** lists signify the life and energy of these bells – symbolic of the change that has taken place in Scrooge.

## Sentence structure

Dickens uses a great variety of sentence structures in *A Christmas Carol*. Some sentences are very long – a feature typical of 19th-century writing, although it is less common in modern novels. The paragraph describing the grocers is a good example of this. It begins with a relatively short sentence and is followed by two very long sentences. Both of these are packed with descriptive detail, designed to create a sense of the abundance associated with the season and the eagerness and excitement of the customers on Christmas morning.

Dickens also often uses short sentences for dramatic impact. When the Ghost of Christmas Past tells Scrooge of the solitary child in the school, '**Scrooge said he knew it. And he sobbed.**' The three-word sentence emphasises Scrooge's emotional response – one of the first indications that he is capable of feeling sadness. What other short sentences can you find in the story? Why do you think Dickens has used them where he has?

## DEVELOP AND REVISE

### Investigating imagery

**1** Explain how Dickens uses imagery in the following cases. For each one, describe its effect.

> And when he thought that such another creature, quite as graceful and as full of promise, might have called him father, and been a springtime in the haggard winter of his life, his sight grew very dim indeed.

Stave Two

> There were ruddy, brown-faced, broad-girthed Spanish onions, shining in the fatness of their growth like Spanish Friars, winking from their shelves in wanton slyness, at the girls as they went by and glanced demurely at the hung-up mistletoe.

Stave Three

> Great heaps of seaweed clung to its base, and storm birds – born of the wind, one might suppose, as seaweed of the water – rose and fell about it, like the waves they skimmed.

Stave Three

**2** Choose one of the following paragraphs and examine Dickens's use of language in it. Depending on your choice, you could focus on:

a   the narrative voice
b   detail
c   vocabulary and/or imagery
d   variation of sentence structures
e   use of listing and/or repetition
f   anything else you consider to be of interest.

- **Stave One:** from '**Meanwhile the fog and darkness thickened so**' to '**while his lean wife and the baby sallied out to buy the beef**'.
- **Stave Two:** from '**But now a knocking at the door was heard**' to '**where they went to bed, and so subsided**'.
- **Stave Three:** from '**Such a bustle ensued**' to '**and feebly cried Hurrah!**'
- **Stave Four:** from '**Far in this den of infamous resort**' to '**all the luxury of calm retirement**'.

No warmth could
warm, no wintry
weather chill him.

*Stave One*

# Preparing for your exam

## WHAT THE EXAM REQUIRES

For your GCSE in English Literature, you will be assessed on *A Christmas Carol* in **Section B** of **Paper 1: Shakespeare and the 19th-century novel**. Paper 1 lasts for 1 hour and 45 minutes, and is worth 40% of your GCSE in English Literature. You have just over 50 minutes for your answer on *A Christmas Carol*.

You will have to answer one question on *A Christmas Carol*. You will be required to write in detail about an extract from the novel that is printed in your exam paper and then to write about the novel as a whole. The question is worth 30 marks.

The first part of the question will make clear the part of the text provided, and the subject to be focused on. Then there will be two bullet points, emphasising that the answer should be based on the extract and on the novel as a whole.

The format of the question is like this:

**In an extract from (Stave X), Dickens describes (person, situation, event, place, relationship, emotions, etc.). Write about:**

- **how Dickens presents the (person, situation, event, place, relationship, emotions, etc.) in the extract**
- **how the (person, situation, event, place, relationship, emotions, etc.) are presented in the novel as a whole.**

## The assessment objective skills

Your answers will be assessed against three assessment objectives (AOs) – skills that you are expected to show. Notice the marks for each assessment objective and take account of this as you manage your time and focus your response.

- **AO1:** Read, understand and write about what happens in the novel, referring to the text and using relevant quotations. (12 marks)
- **AO2:** Analyse the language, form and structure used by Dickens to create meanings and effects. (12 marks)
- **AO3:** Show an understanding of the context of the novel. This might include, depending on the question, when Dickens wrote the novel, the period in which he set the novel and why it was set then, its relevance to readers then and to you in the 21st century. (6 marks)

# Planning and responding to a question

Read the practice question and the annotations.

**Charles Dickens:** *A Christmas Carol*

Read the following extract from Stave One and then answer the question that follows.

> *In this extract Scrooge is being introduced to the reader.*
>
> External heat and cold had little influence on Scrooge. No warmth could warm, nor wintry weather chill him. No wind that blew was bitterer than he, no falling snow was more intent upon its purpose, no pelting rain less open to entreaty. Foul weather didn't know where to have him. The heaviest rain, and snow, and hail, and sleet, could boast of the advantage over him in only one respect. They often 'came down' handsomely, and Scrooge never did.
>
> Nobody ever stopped him in the street to say, with gladsome looks, 'My dear Scrooge, how are you? when will you come to see me?' No beggars implored him to bestow a trifle, no children asked him what it was o'clock, no man or woman ever once in all his life inquired the way to such and such a place, of Scrooge. Even the blindmen's dogs appeared to know him; and when they saw him coming on, would tug their owners into doorways and up courts; and then would wag their tails as though they said, 'no eye at all is better than an evil eye, dark master!'
>
> But what did Scrooge care? It was the very thing he liked. To edge his way along the crowded paths of life, warning all human sympathy to keep its distance, was what the knowing ones call 'nuts' to Scrooge.

Starting with this extract, how does Dickens present Scrooge as an outsider to society? Write about:

- how Dickens presents Scrooge in this extract
- how Dickens presents Scrooge as an outsider to society in the novel as a whole.

**[30 marks]**

*Annotations:*

- Lists features of weather to show reader what Scrooge is like.
- Even the worst weather cannot get at him.
- Pun: applied to the weather this means 'fell freely'; in slang it means that someone is free with their money.
- Repetition of 'no' used for emphasis of things that do not happen.
- Extreme example for emphasis – even the dogs avoid him.
- Suggests Scrooge is evil.
- Verb suggests he lives cautiously, on the 'edge' of life.
- Scrooge avoids others and wants them to avoid him
- This originally meant agreeable or good luck.
- As well as considering detail, you need to analyse the language, form and structure used by Dickens to create meanings and effects. (AO1, AO2)
- Rhetorical question used for effect.
- Start with a close reference to the text in the printed extract before widening your response to the novel as a whole. (AO1, AO2)
- This asks you to include contextual elements – in this case, the idea of 'society'. (AO3)

93

## Plan your answer

When planning your answer to any question, focus on three key areas:

- What do you know about the characters, events and ideas at this stage – in this extract and in the novel as a whole? (AO1)
- What comments can you make about how Dickens uses language and style, using examples from this extract? (AO2)
- What is relevant in this extract that relates to the context of the novel as a whole? (AO3)

Look at this example of a student's plan, then explore the example paragraphs and development of skills in writing for GCSE English Literature that follow.

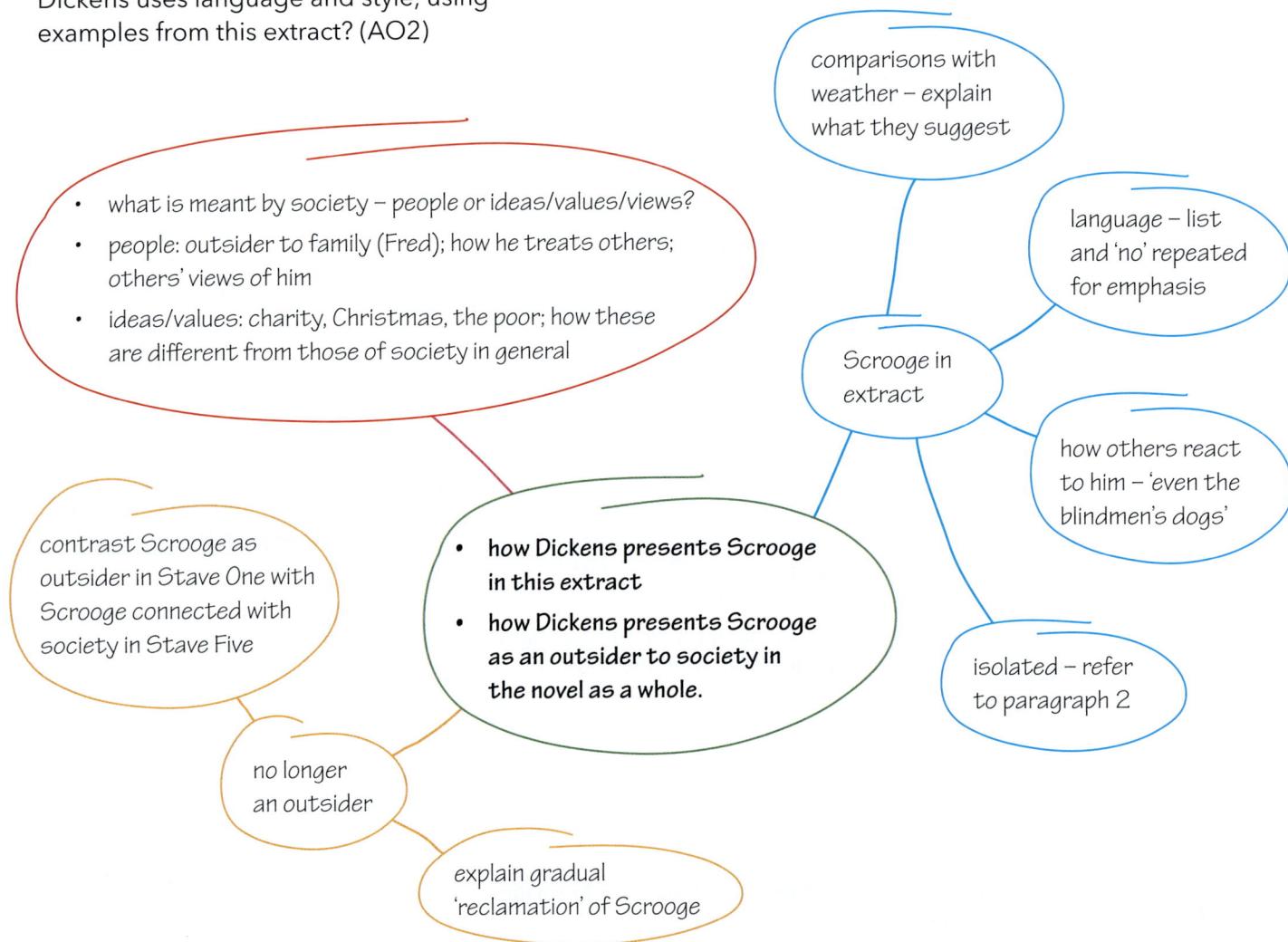

comparisons with weather – explain what they suggest

language – list and 'no' repeated for emphasis

Scrooge in extract

how others react to him – 'even the blindmen's dogs'

isolated – refer to paragraph 2

- what is meant by society – people or ideas/values/views?
- people: outsider to family (Fred); how he treats others; others' views of him
- ideas/values: charity, Christmas, the poor; how these are different from those of society in general

- **how Dickens presents Scrooge in this extract**
- **how Dickens presents Scrooge as an outsider to society in the novel as a whole.**

contrast Scrooge as outsider in Stave One with Scrooge connected with society in Stave Five

no longer an outsider

explain gradual 'reclamation' of Scrooge

### Remember:

✔ **More competent answers** will explore Dickens's craft and purpose in creating the character of Scrooge and showing his relationship with society. They will connect his actions to the writer's ideas and to the effects on the reader. They will offer a personal response and many well-explained details.

✔ **Good answers** will show a clear understanding of how Dickens develops the character of Scrooge and his relationship with society, using well-chosen examples.

✔ **Weaker answers** will only explain what happens to Scrooge and the relationship between Scrooge and some other characters, without using many examples or mentioning how Dickens presents them.

## Show your skills

To help you think about your own writing, look at these six example paragraphs of writing about *A Christmas Carol*, and the different range of skills displayed in each paragraph.

Scrooge is a man whose partner Marley has died. He is not a very nice man. He is very cold and no one goes near him, not even a dog.

> Some simple facts stated.

Scrooge is a very cold man and 'no warmth could warm him'. No child or beggar ever goes near him. Everyone stays away from him. It says that 'Even the blindmen's dogs' keep away from him.

> Statement supported with quotation.

This is the first time that Scrooge is described in detail, and Dickens presents him as a cold and distant figure who is not affected by even the most 'foul weather'. Dickens helps the reader understand what he is like by showing that no one goes near him, not 'even the blindmen's dogs'. He likes to be on his own, which is very different from how he is at the end of the story.

> Explanation structured by reference to writer, reader and other parts of the text.

Dickens describes Scrooge as a man who is isolated from society. This is first shown by the references to the weather. No wind is 'bitterer than he' and 'no pelting rain less open to entreaty'. The reader is told that people keep away from him, such as the beggars and the children. Not even the 'blindmen's dogs' will go near him, but Scrooge is not bothered. He 'liked' people to keep their distance – it was what he wanted.

> Provides a range of detail to keep clearly illustrating a point.

Dickens shows that Scrooge is not affected by anything that happens around him. The weather has no effect on him and he is 'less open to entreaty' than the 'pelting rain'. He lives in his own little world, wanting no connection with 'human sympathy'. The point that 'even the blindmen's dogs' steer their masters away from him suggests that he has no empathy at all with others, even those who most need kindness and assistance. He lacks the ability to relate to others, and others steer well clear of him.

> Uses details to develop an interpretation, going beyond what the text states explicitly.

It is significant that Scrooge chooses his isolation: 'It was the very thing he liked'. Dickens suggests that his normal human feelings have been stunted by the cold within him. He is so intent on his 'purpose' that nothing else has an impact on his self-created world. The weather cannot distract him; he is fiercer than it can ever be, so fierce that people and 'even the blindmen's dogs' avoid approaching him. Such isolation is portrayed as unnatural, the consequence of a determined and calculated withdrawal from the world.

> An argued interpretation that includes references to writer, contexts and ideas.

## Plan and write your own response

Now plan and write your own response to the practice question. You can then assess your skills against the example responses that follow.

✔ **Complete this assignment on Cambridge Elevate.**

## ASSESS YOUR SKILLS

The following extracts are from sample responses to the practice question. They provide examples of skills at different levels when writing for GCSE English Literature.

Use these examples to assess your own skills in responding to the practice question so that you know what you do well and can focus on areas to improve.

Compare the responses with your own answer to the question. As you read the responses, think about how far each example – and your own answer – is successful in:

- sustaining focus on the question
- supporting comment with textual detail
- making use of textual detail to build interpretation
- linking detail with Dickens's craft in writing a novel and his purpose in conveying characters, relationships and ideas.

### Student A

This is taken from early in Student A's response:

Scrooge is clearly an outsider to society in this extract. The weather has no effect on him because he is already cold inside, which means that he doesn't have a warm heart. He never gives anything to anyone and everyone avoids him all the time. Dickens lists all the people who avoid him, like the children and the beggars and says that 'even the blindmen's dogs' kept away from him to show that even animals won't go near him. Scrooge quite likes it this way as he doesn't want to get involved with anyone. He likes to keep himself to himself. He doesn't care that people don't talk to him and he likes not having anyone ask him for anything.

> Links to the task.
>
> Shows understanding of meaning.
>
> Mentions the writer and shows awareness of a particular technique.
>
> Selects a quotation to support a point.
>
> Shows understanding of character.

This is taken from further on in Student A's response:

In the story Scrooge doesn't really get on well with anyone. He argues with his nephew, Fred, and is mean to his clerk, Bob Cratchit. He's also mean with his money and won't give anything to the carol singer or the men collecting for the poor. When Marley's Ghost arrives, it tells him that he needs to make 'mankind his business' so that he won't have to carry a long chain when he dies. As the story goes on Scrooge starts to get a bit more involved in society, because the Ghost of Christmas Present takes him to see how Christmas is spent in poor homes. It also shows him the bad things that happen to children because people like Scrooge have ignored them.

In these parts of the response, Student A engages with the character as a real person, rather than as a character created by the writer. The response shows:

- understanding of character, but not characterisation
- some awareness of the writer's method
- use of textual detail to support simple comment
- awareness of Scrooge's attitudes and actions
- awareness of Scrooge's development in the course of the story
- some focus on the task.

**1** Work in pairs. Annotate the second paragraph of Student A's answer to see if you can find more examples of the same skills, or any new ones.

**2** Talk together about what you think is good about the answer.

**3** Look carefully at the three assessment objectives. What advice would you give Student A on how to improve this answer?

## Student B

This is taken from early in Student B's response:

Dickens uses images of harsh weather to help the reader picture Scrooge. He emphasises the coldness of his heart by explaining how 'no wintry wind could chill him'. He characterises him as bitter, intent on purpose and not open to entreaty by using the elements of wind, snow and rain. In the second paragraph, Dickens shows how no one will approach Scrooge by listing the different types of people who keep away from him. He repeatedly uses the word 'no' to give emphasis to this list. The word 'even' is used to break the pattern and draw the reader's attention to the fact that animals also avoid Scrooge. It makes it seem as though he has no contact with society at all, but then Dickens tells us that this is 'the very thing he liked'. He uses the verb 'edge' to suggest that Scrooge is on the very outside of society but that this is where he wants to be.

> Shows understanding of the writer's purpose.

> Selects quotation to support a point.

> Shows understand of how language is used and the effect it has.

> Discusses Scrooge as a character, not a real person.

This is taken from further on in Student B's response:

In Stave Two, Dickens shows the reader that Scrooge was not always an outsider to society. He had friends at school, a sister who loved him, a kind and generous employer and a fiancée. It was his break with Belle that, Dickens suggests, marked the final break with society and denied Scrooge the chance for a happy life. As he became increasingly obsessed with his business, he became harsh and uncaring about others. His condemnation of the poor and destitute to the workhouses and the prisons – places of great suffering in the early 19th century – shows how little he understands or empathises with the lives of others. He is, however, forced to rethink his own distorted views on society, when he meets the children Want and Ignorance in Stave Three and the Ghost uses his own words against him: 'Are there no prisons? Are there no workhouses?'

This is a stronger response than Student A's. In these parts of the response, Student B is clearly focused on the author's craft and purpose. The response engages with character and relationship. It includes personal interpretation. It shows:

- understanding of Dickens's characterisation
- understanding of and comment on features of language
- reference to the text and use of relevant quotation
- sustained comment on meaning of textual detail
- understanding of contextual detail, exemplified in reference to the suffering in workhouses
- focus on task.

**1** Work in pairs. Annotate the second paragraph of Student B's answer to see if you can find more examples of the same skills, or any new ones.

**2** Talk together about what you think is good about the answer.

**3** Look carefully at the three assessment objectives. What advice would you give Student B on how to improve this answer?

## Student C

This is taken from early in Student C's response:

This extract reveals the narrator's – and through him Dickens's – judgement on Scrooge. In many ways it develops and explains an earlier simile, in which Scrooge is described as being 'solitary as an oyster'. Scrooge is shown to be impervious to the elements of weather. Not only this, but through the comparisons with the elements of wind, 'falling snow' and 'pelting rain' – images that the reader can readily identify with – Dickens shows Scrooge to be more severe.

| Shows understanding of perspective. |
| Links with an earlier part of the text. |
| Describes effect on the reader. |

The sequence signalled by the repeated use of 'no' is effectively continued in the following paragraph, as Dickens lists the beggars, children, men and women who avoid contact with Scrooge. A society is generally closely associated with its people and, whilst Scrooge may repel the weather, it is the people who are more significant. Their instinctive avoidance of him is shown by Dickens's reference to the 'blindmen's dogs' who steer away from his 'evil eye'. The **alliteration** of this phrase combined with its connotations of black magic gives emphasis to how Scrooge is viewed by even the most helpless.

| Shows understanding of structure and how sections are linked. |
| Refers back to the question asked. |
| Uses short quotations to support a point. |
| Shows understanding of purpose. |

Anticipating the reader's response, Dickens raises and answers the rhetorical question 'But what did Scrooge care?', using a metaphorical image to reveal that Scrooge chose this life. The verb 'to edge' suggests that Scrooge has a cautious, perhaps even nervous approach to life, whilst the 'crowded paths of life' is suggestive of the people and society that Marley later reveals should have been his business.

| Makes effective use of technical term. |
| Looks forward to a later point in the text. |

This is taken from further on in Student C's response:

In Stave One, Dickens uses the two portly gentlemen to convey his disapproval of the workhouses and prisons, the only refuge of the poor and destitute. Scrooge, in his response that he does enough by paying his taxes, is, perhaps, not so distant from others in Victorian society who readily distinguished between the 'deserving' and the 'idle' poor. The Ghost of Christmas Past shows him what he has forgotten – how to feel joy, sadness and remorse; it is necessary for Scrooge to reconnect with human feelings, both his own and those of others, if he is to reconnect with society.

Dickens also throws new light on Scrooge's disassociation with society in Stave Two. Belle tells him 'you fear the world too much' and the possibility of its 'sordid reproach', the adjective here emphasising Belle's views (and through her, Dickens's views) on the merits of this world view. She suggests that his focus on 'gain' is in some way an attempt to protect himself from a world that condemns poverty, to create a barrier between himself and the society in which he lives. Here, Dickens suggests to the reader a more vulnerable side to Scrooge. It is ironic then that such a man, having built his barrier of wealth, is himself the harshest judge of those who lack it.

This is the best of the three responses. It shows:

- understanding of characterisation and the writer's purpose
- comment with analysis of language features
- well-used textual detail to support the points made
- exploration of the writer's ideas
- understanding of contextual viewpoints
- a good focus on the task.

**1** Comment on the ways in which Student C:

**a** understands what the extract is about – its ideas and importance in the novel

**b** explains the effect of the extract on the reader and shows why it has that effect

**c** uses quotations from the extract as evidence to support an argument and does not just put forward opinions without any support

**d** looks at the whole extract and does not get stuck on one part of it

**e** shows a knowledge of the context in which the novel was written and how it might be received by 21st-century readers

**f** convincingly explores and evaluates one or more of the ideas in the text as a whole.

---

**🔑 Key terms**

**alliteration:** the repetition of a sound for effect at the beginning of adjacent words.

# Practice questions

Use your learning in this section to create practice questions and develop your skills further.

**1** Work with another student to:

   **a**   choose a topic from the list in this section, or a topic of your choice

   **b**   choose a suitable extract of around 300 words

   **c**   create your practice questions.

Use these prompts to create your question:

- choose a suitable extract
- choose a suitable topic
- choose a focus for writing about the extract.

Your question should look like this:

---

**Starting with this extract, write about how Dickens presents (your choice of topic). Write about:**

- **how Dickens presents (your choice of focus) in this extract**
- **how Dickens presents (your choice of topic) in the novel as a whole.**

---

> **Topics**
> - the ghosts
> - poverty and the poor
> - the Cratchit family
> - minor characters
> - Christmas
> - business
> - children and childhood.

**2** Now answer the question, using the skills you have developed. As you plan and write, think about how far you:

   **a**   sustain your focus on the question

   **b**   support comments with textual detail

   **c**   make use of textual detail to build interpretation

   **d**   link detail with Dickens's craft in writing the novel and his purpose in conveying characters and ideas.

**3** Swap work with your partner. Using these points and your work in this section, comment on the skills shown in the answer. Suggest three areas that could be improved.

✔ **Complete this assignment on Cambridge Elevate.**

The spirit gazed upon him mildly. Its gentle touch [...] appeared still present to the old man's sense of feeling.

*Stave Two*

# Glossary

**adjective** a word that describes a person, place or thing

**adverb** a word that adds to the meaning of a verb, adjective or other adverb

**allegory** a story, poem or painting in which the apparent meaning of the characters and events is used to symbolise a deeper moral or spiritual meaning

**alliteration** the repetition of a sound for effect at the beginning of adjacent words

**allusion** a reference to something that the listener or reader will recognise

**antonym** a word with opposite meaning to another

**characterise** to describe features that are unique or distinctive

**characters** the people in a story; even when based on real people, characters in a novel are invented or fictionalised

**connotations** things or ideas suggested by a word

**context** the historical circumstances of a piece of writing, which affect what an author wrote and the way they wrote it

**contrast** the way in which two or more things are different from one another

**dialogue** a conversation between two or more people in a piece of writing

**dramatic irony** when the reader or audience knows something that a character in a novel or play does not

**first-person narrative** an account of events using the pronouns 'I', 'me' and 'we'

**genre** the kind or type of literature to which a text belongs; stories within a particular genre will have similar characteristics

**imagery** language intended to conjure up a vivid picture in the reader's mind

**juxtapose** to place two ideas or things near each other to invite comparison or contrast

**metaphor** a type of comparison that describes one thing as if it was another

**narrator** the character in a novel who tells the story

**noun phrase** a group of words that function as a noun

**novella** a literary term for a work that is too long to be a short story, but shorter than a conventional novel

**onomatopoeic** describing a word whose sound suggests its meaning

**personification** a type of metaphor that gives human qualities to inanimate objects

**preface** an introduction or explanation written by the author at the start of a book

**simile** a comparison between two things that uses the words 'as' or 'like'

**symbol** an object used to represent something else

**theme** an idea that a writer keeps returning to, exploring it from different perspectives

**third-person narrative** an account of events using 'he', 'she' or 'they', rather than 'I' or 'we'

**tone** the mood or attitude that a writer conveys in a story

# Acknowledgements

## Picture credits

cover plainpicture/Monika Kluza, © 2013 Fabian Oefner www.FabianOefner.com; p. 5 (t) Elliott Franks/ArenaPAL/Topfoto; p. 5 (b) nickolae/ Fotolia; p. 7 Pete Jones/ArenaPAL/Topfoto; p. 11 UPP/Topfoto; p. 12 HLPhoto/Fotolia; p. 13 Donald Cooper/Photostage; p. 17 AF Archive/Alamy; p. 21 Photos.com/Thinkstock; p. 23 Lebrecht Music and Arts Photo Library/Alamy; p. 24 nasared/Fotolia; p. 25 Donald Cooper/Photostage; p. 29 Lebrecht Music and Arts Photo Library/Alamy; p. 31 Jean Auvinet/Fotolia; p. 33 AF Archive/Alamy; p. 34 Michael Ward/ArenaPAL/Topfoto; p. 36 Springfield Gallery/Fotolia; p. 37 Elliott Franks/ArenaPAL/ Topfoto; p. 41 drhfoto/Fotolia; p. 45 AF Archive/ Alamy; p. 47 World History Archive/Alamy; p. 49 AF Archive/Alamy; p. 50 Tamas Zsebok/Fotolia; p. 51 Classic Stock/Alamy; p. 53 Linda Rich/ ArenaPAL/Topfoto; p. 57 Anthony Hall/Fotolia; p. 60 Petoo/Fotolia; p. 61 AF Archive/Alamy; p. 63 Marilyn Kingwill/ArenaPAL/Topfoto; p. 65 kamera7/Fotolia; p. 69 ZUMA Press Inc./Alamy; p. 70 davidetrolli/Fotolia; p. 73 AF Archive/Alamy; p. 75 Lebrecht Music and Arts Photo Library/ Alamy; p. 76 Chorazin/Fotolia; p. 78 AF Archive/ Alamy; p. 80 Larry Lilac/Alamy; p. 83 Marilyn Kingwill/ArenaPAL/Topfoto; p. 84 Pefkos/Fotolia; p. 86 Nigel Norrington/ArenaPAL/Topfoto; p. 88 Marilyn Kingwill/ArenaPAL/Topfoto; p. 91 Nigel Norrington/ArenaPAL/Topfoto; p. 92 Pete Jones/ ArenaPAL/Topfoto; p. 101 AF Archive/Alamy.

Produced for Cambridge University Press by

White-Thomson Publishing
www.wtpub.co.uk

Editor: Sonya Newland
Designer: Clare Nicholas